FROM THE
LIBRARY OF

DOUBLEDAY & COMPANY, INC.
GARDEN CITY, NEW YORK
1975

HELEN VAN PELT WILSON
SUCCESSFUL
GARDENING
IN
THE SHADE

WITH GRATITUDE

To Rachel Snyder, Editor-in-Chief of *Flower and Garden,* for permitting me to draw on articles I had written for that magazine about my shaded plantings.

To William L. Meacham, Managing Editor of *Natural Gardening,* for permission to use the chapter "Shade" that appeared in that magazine.

FRONTIS FLOWERS

Above: Left, Pink speciosum lilies;
Right, White foamflower
Center: Yellow petticoat narcissus
Below: Left, Yellow winter aconites;
Right, Yellow polyantha primroses

LIBRARY OF CONGRESS CATALOGING IN PUBLICATION DATA

WILSON, HELEN VAN PELT, 1901–
SUCCESSFUL GARDENING IN THE SHADE.

I.   GARDENING IN THE SHADE.   I.   TITLE.
SB454.W693   635.9'54
ISBN 0-385-08629-6
LIBRARY OF CONGRESS CATALOG CARD NUMBER 74–10384

BOOK DESIGN BY BENTE HAMANN

FOR
JOAN ROOT
A LOYAL AND DEVOTED FRIEND

CONTENTS

Charts and Lists

Where'er you walk cool gales shall fan the glade;
Trees where you sit shall crowd into a shade.
Where'er you tread, the blushing flowers shall rise,
And all things flourish, where'er you turn your eyes.

FROM HANDEL'S *Semele*

POEM BY WILLIAM CONGREVE

PLEASURES
OF A SHADED PLACE

It was the summer the marigolds failed in the bed under the kitchen casements and the zinnias and pinks put on a meager show along the driveway that it dawned on me that my way of gardening was due for a change. It was more than twenty years since I had first come to my glaringly sunny cottage, and through those years and in that time I had been busy planting all kinds of sun-loving annuals, perennials, shrubs, and trees—lots of them, big shade ones and smaller flowering kinds. The sweetgum and ash on the southeast corner of the house and a European birch to the south of the terrace had now grown mightily shading house and entrance. Elsewhere silverbell, fringetree, goldenrain, and dogwood were no longer slim youngsters but adults of obvious girth that restrained the sun from the plantings beneath.

So much tree planting had now led somewhat unexpectedly—though why I should have been surprised I cannot say—to my having to garden today almost exclusively in shade. But what a pleasure this is, the sunstruck surround of my cottage now a shaded oasis. Such comfort, quiet, and serenity in summer when the house becomes a cool cavern. If you have been fretting over your shady place, consider what your trees are doing for you—actually they cool, really air-condition the atmosphere, and also mitigate noise. "Is it air-conditioned?" your guests may ask. "No, tree-conditioned," you can tell them.

I have also discovered that one of the lovely dividends of shade is *shadow*—the straight bare trunk of the oak tree casting tremulous patterns on the coruscated surface of the rock cliff; the long dark bars of balm tree, sweetgum, and ash bisecting the open sunny stretch of the small front lawn; the four-stemmed white birch projecting giant prongs across the driveway, and these shadows, blue in winter on white snow, are then as exciting as in summer.

If you are unhappy because yours is a too-shaded place with meager grass and little bloom, don't think you must endure it so. Since nature abhors a vacuum, you may too, only you can be more selective than nature and plant what you like with due regard, of course, for the kind of shade your property offers. Only, please, don't consider shade a problem. It isn't. Gardening in the shade is simply different from gardening in the sun; your objectives are different; other kinds of plants must be considered.

I think of my clump of snow trilliums under a box-elder, the marsh-marigolds and daffodils across the brook shadowed by the cliff, a circle of white hostas under a dogwood tree, patches of yellow trout-lilies and winter aconites in the woods, evergreen leucothoe and andromedas beneath a sugar maple, and a whole garden of bleedinghearts and Virginia bluebells and other spring treasures like a carpet under the old apple tree. Of course, spring bulbs, especially narcissus, are everywhere, pink and blue hyacinths at the back door, and quantities of peonies, daylilies, and balloon-flowers in many half-shade, half-sun locations.

Indeed, you need be neither limited nor deprived when you

garden in shade. For you, too, shade will mean cool summer rooms and a pleasant sense of serenity—all this so much more agreeable in hot weather than a great blazing expanse of red and orange flowers flashing at you; at least, it seems so to me. But then I am no devotee of the burning beach or the sun bath elsewhere. I prefer the shaded terrace, the screened porch, and an environment that alleviates the rigors of summer.

Let me now share with you the pleasures of my own shaded place and the means by which they were achieved. Sometimes it took a little doing, so forward, let us go.

HELEN VAN PELT WILSON
FEBRUARY 1974

In the open shade of tall trees, well-chosen evergreen shrubs, rhododendrons, and dwarf boxwood make a narrow pathway garden along the side of a house. PAUL E. GENEREUX PHOTO

WHAT KIND OF SHADE HAVE YOU?

Dense, Light, Half-and-Half, or "Sky Shine"

Even my dictionary has trouble with the word shade, and there no helpful horticultural statement is expected. I rather like "comparative obscurity" because when I try to define shade that would seem to be where I am. Absence of sunlight would be a simple, true, but only moderately useful guideline for us gardeners. Perhaps it will be best for me to try to analyze the different kinds of shade I have here at Stony Brook Cottage, and tell you how I have handled them.

Dense Shade

An old stand of hemlocks and pines produces this deep shade along the boundaries and view-blocking places beside the driveway. I am told that pachysandra will grow even here but I prefer the

In half-and-half shade, with more shadow than sunlight, ferns, hostas, and epimedium thrive with yews against a tall background of viburnums. GEORGE TALOUMIS PHOTO

Light alone reaches my Round Garden now that the background trees have grown so tall. Petunias used to bloom here but now for flowers I only count on a fine pink-and-lavender spring display of wood-hyacinths, *Scilla hispanica,* and white summer hostas amidst the enduring green of Christmas ferns. MOLLY ADAMS PHOTO

natural look of a deep needle mulch and attempt no planting underneath. However, in a woodland setting, hemlocks and pines offer perfect conditions for pink lady-slippers and trailing arbutus that require the special fungus existing in the soil in which these evergreens grow.

Perhaps your house is closely shaded by old overgrown evergreens that cut off light and air and force you to keep lights on inside even in winter. There are ways to deal with most kinds of shade but not this one. You just have to remove your antique "foundation planting" and substitute dwarf material that knows its place under windows, not in front of them. (This is not always an easy business; for some reason men sometimes carry on about such "destruction." I thought my lawyer was going to demand a divorce when he came upon men with power saws and spades cutting down the scrawny yews and hemlocks beside his doorway—alas, at my suggestion.) Really there is no way to handle dense shade right next to the house except by removing the cause.

Elsewhere perhaps great trees of truly noble aspect now shut out the sun completely and the ground is bare in their dense shade. Here with some little effort at soil improvement, you can successfully grow English ivy, pachysandra, moneywort, of course, and perhaps such ferns as the Christmas. However, if you yearn for flowers I fear you will have to be selective and remove a big tree or two. (Don't stay home the day the men do the cutting; too painful, but very worthwhile.) Buildings or walls close by may have the same subduing effect. But where deep shade is cast only in summer, as from beech, chestnut, catalpa, and maple, you could plant with effort a late-winter-early-spring garden with bulbs and perennials that have no need for summer light. In Chapters 5 and 7 let's think about these grand possibilities.

Light Shade

This is the nice comfortable kind you can sit under on a hot summer day or make a flower garden underneath with plants that

Here is the nice comfortable kind of shade you can sit under on a hot summer day. Shifting sunlight comes through the branches of this deep-rooted, high-pruned oak for the benefit of potted tuberous begonias, yews, cotoneasters, and mahonia beneath. GEORGE TALOUMIS PHOTO

need only a little shifting sunlight. Deep-rooted deciduous trees—ash, oak, sweet gum, and honeylocust—bare in winter and spring but open enough for shifting sunshine to come through in summer and fall—make excellent situations for summer-flowering perennials—astilbes, balloon-flowers, daylilies—as well as early spring bulbs. Under apple, wild cherry, pin oak, birch, Christmas-berry,

An ancient crab apple shades a rhododendron clump and part of an edging of impatiens but does not keep the sunlight from reaching the raised tubs of geraniums just beyond. GEORGE TALOUMIS PHOTO

and thorn-tree, I've grown a wealth of flowering plants, and in one area developed a woodland garden, first thinning out some of the trees there. I've also managed flowers under maples on a dry root-ridden bank. (See Color Section.) But here I am getting rather ahead of myself into variables of soil and moisture that I want to talk about later. Pruning, too, is most important for you can actu-

Along the east side of a house where only early sunshine strikes a narrow border, a white dogwood shades a bluestone bench and rhododendrons flourish in a bed of pachysandra.
GEORGE TALOUMIS PHOTO

ally "make" a plantable kind of shade by high and open pruning of big trees and then have all the flowers you want, though, of course, not all kinds. Some are much more sun-dependent than others, most of the vast daisy clan, for instance.

Half-shade, Half-sun

Places with four to five hours each of sun and shade offer endless possibilities; even when the division isn't equal and with more

This narrow walk between
houses is open to the sky.
At right, where only a little
morning sun strikes, George
Taloumis grows spicebush,
azaleas, hostas, and
canterbury-bells with an
edging of lambs-ears and
lamium as groundcovers;
at left, rhododendrons,
azaleas, junipers, euonymus,
and dwarf yew rise from a
bed of Baltic ivy.

At this doorway there is constant shade; the terrace facing east gets some morning sun but is cool and shaded by afternoon when it is pleasant to sit there. The wisteria vine decorates but will not bloom except above where it gets adequate sunshine. PAUL E. GENEREUX PHOTO

shade than sun. On one side of my driveway that runs northeast, only a couple of hours of morning sun strike the crab-apple tree, the big viburnums, and the peonies; then the sun moves across tall trees and shrubs to the south where petunias bloom at the sunny *edge* of the shaded bed and Christmas-roses flourish in considerable shade underneath birch and silverbell trees. Perhaps you have the reverse, with morning shade and afternoon sun. Both situations offer considerable opportunity, although the late sun is not so strong as that of the early hours. When I have this condition,

A rocky slope in open shade is beautifully planted with patches of pale blue phlox, white epimedium, and white hardy candytuft beside the path and white azalea bushes at the top close to the high-pruned tree. PAUL E. GENEREUX PHOTO

azaleas and tree peonies do well with only a few hours of sunlight. On the west, where the rocky cliff cuts off the late sunshine, Oregon holly-grape gets enough to bloom well, and also the August lilies. The silverlace-vine liked the site so well it threatened the safety of the house and had to be removed.

Most sun-lovers will bloom *moderately* in half-shade, half-sun situations, but if you plant trees that bloom before they leaf out, as shadbush, redbud, dogwood, and benzoin, you will get more satisfactory flowering of the plants underneath.

Light Only

This is what that excellent gardener Lois Wilson calls "sky shine," that is, full light but no sun. Under this condition of light from above but pretty thick shade below, even lilacs bloom well at the top for me. Then I have seen charming garden plots along the narrow north side of a property where a neighbor's house or fence blocked out the sun but there was plenty of overhead light. If you have this situation, don't just fill up the area with trash cans and attic discards. Plant a little garden there. Make a path of narrow flagstones or shiny white pebbles that attract the light. Ferns and early spring bulbs will flourish. Or along the path you might work out a small balanced design edged with one of the dwarf varieties of candytuft like 'Purity' and use the shade-tolerant annual impatiens, an Elfin pink or white perhaps, for bedding. Many north-facing rather narrow city yards have been so transformed and bring forth a surprising succession of spring-to-autumn blossoms with evergreen foliage all year. In any case, as you look at the pictures in this book, please keep in mind that the photographer needs sunlight for maximum effect. Hence some pictures were taken during the often brief period when the sun shone upon the planting or a part of it.

It comes down to this. Whatever kind of shade or light you have, probably some of each as I have, and maybe one place where a long border moves from full sun to considerable shade, you can do something beautiful with it. First, you need to evaluate your conditions and their possibilities; then you will probably have to get involved in what I call my Four Basic Practices that are coming up next.

High-pruned, deep-rooted
trees bring serene summer
comfort to a dwelling and
cast lovely shadows upon a
lawn of fine shade grasses.
GEORGE TALOUMIS PHOTO

FOUR BASIC PRACTICES
FOR SHADY SUCCESS

Pruning, Fertility,
Moisture, and Mulch

If shade has been your problem instead of your pleasure—as it
should and can be—why not examine your whole situation to see
what needs changing? Perhaps you are overplanted, particularly
if yours is an old property where the trees, and these may be
choice kinds, have taken over. Crowding destroys their own beauty
and usefulness and inevitably prevents most plants beneath them
from blooming. Perhaps your shrubs have grown out of control—
rampant forsythias fighting it out with mighty mock-oranges and
neither blooming very well. When you look out of your windows,
do you see thickets or vistas? Well, proper pruning can change all
this.

Pruning to the Rescue

Consider first what proper pruning could do for your big shade
trees. Try to visualize what the effect would be of removing certain
heavy limbs, perhaps clearing trunks up to 30 feet, as I have on all

the front-lawn trees, and opening up tops to develop a fine silhouette instead of the present shapeless mounds. Will such a stern procedure let in too much sun where you don't want it or reveal a view of your neighbor's outdoor housekeeping that you'd prefer not to see, or maybe destroy your privacy? Take your time; think it out not in a day but perhaps in the course of a week or so.

When it comes to an extensive pruning job on trees that have long gone their own sweet way, you had better employ the services of a good tree man. Since spraying may also be part of his business, he will probably be terribly busy in spring. Of course, you can arrange for your work well ahead so that he can allow time for you then, but I have found that July is a dandy time for pruning. Most trees can be pruned in midsummer when the tree man is freer and so am I, the tasks of spring clean-up and fertilizing completed by that month.

Try to pick a patient tree-man like mine, who won't object if you change your mind occasionally as he works and you actually see the results. Anyway, don't hurry him. Together, his skill and your vision must be synchronized. When the work is done, your trees should look shaped and beautiful, not butchered, lopsided, or top-sheared. No basal suckers should remain, no weak leaf clusters, only a clear silhouette of trunks. If pruning has not been attended to on a yearly or biyearly schedule, don't try to do it all at once. After the leaves fall, the opened-up silhouette should have a sculptural quality, so you will want to consider the winter as well as the summer effect. I enjoy this whole business of pruning; it means so much to the beauty and comfort of this place, and to me is such an intriguing aspect of gardening.

Once your place is under control, the big pruning job done, over the course of, say, two years, the man of the family with a few proper tools can probably cope without professional help. Watch him though; men can get terribly enthusiastic with nice sharp tools on a pleasant day. You don't want some big favorite reduced to sapling size because energy ran high and the work was fun. Certainly, it *is* fun.

Above. Pruning Shears. Long ago I found it a waste of time to walk about the place without these in hand. I always saw something dead, crooked, or crowded that I wanted to remove, and then I had to come back to the house for my pruners. These shears are useful for small pruning, shaping, and trimming and will cut branches up to ¾-inch thickness on flowering shrubs, evergreens, and trees. *Center.* Lopping Shears. Hook-and-blade or anvil-style loppers can do heavier work than the smaller hand pruners. I use them to remove low limbs I can reach on trees and ornamental shrubs, including laurels and rhododendrons, and for shaping larger evergreens to keep them from crowding and so preventing light from reaching the groundcovers around them. *Below.* Curved Pruning Saw. The blade of this 10-inch saw fits back into the handle for convenient storage. The medium-coarse teeth easily cut branches of more than 1½-inch thickness and make it easy to work where limbs and canes are crowded and you want to do a selective job without damage to nearby growth. SEYMOUR SMITH & SON, INC. PHOTOS

Left. Heavy-Duty Saw. For heavy work, use this strong 22-inch straight saw. Notice how it is aimed to make a clean cut. When the limb is off, a spray or dressing of tree-wound paint will protect the cut from the entrance of disease. *Below*. Pole Pruner and Extension Saw. From the ground, you can reach into a tree 6 to 12 feet above you to saw off small branches; or you can remove the saw and use the hook pruner alone, operating it with pulls of the long cord. For the long and the short of us, this extension of our reach (with no dangerous ladder needed) is a great convenience. SEYMOUR SMITH & SON, INC. PHOTOS

Anyway, a few tools are a necessity for work that doesn't require professional help. I have a hand-pruner and a lopping pruner for the smaller jobs I can manage myself if they are in reach; two saws, one curved and one straight, for work I can direct my by-the-hour man to do (after the big drastic clean-up has been finished), and a pole pruner that can be extended to 12 feet for light but faraway work. (When I can't manage this, my kind tall neighbor helps.) Then an aerosol can of tree paint is essential to cover cuts and prevent the entrance of disease organisms.

Except to urge you to make sharp cuts, to leave no stubs, and to cover all cuts larger than a nickel with tree-wound paint, I won't attempt to explain here the essentials of pruning. You need to know the why, where, and how for each of your trees and shrubs. Actually, pruning is an art, and though what you want to do probably stops short of topiaries and espaliers, you will be wise to give the subject a little study. For shrubs and hardy vines, you have to know which ones produce flowers on new growth, which on last year's growth, and exactly *when* to prune. Young trees should sometimes be pruned properly to prevent the development of weak crotches or strength-sapping lateral branches. The U. S. Department of Agriculture offers two excellent, well-illustrated pamphlets for your guidance: No. 83, "Pruning Shade Trees and Repairing Their Injuries," and No. 165, "Pruning Ornamental Shrubs and Vines." These are for sale, 10 cents each, from the Superintendent of Documents, U. S. Government Printing Office, Washington, D.C. 20402.

Improving Fertility

For success, especially under trees, some soil improvement is essential, but I don't mean a 2-foot excavation. (When I read that recommendation or directions for drainage tile, I simply turn the page; in fact, in all my years of gardening I've never done such

Where shade is heavy or where there is light without sunshine stone mulching can take the place of grass with only an occasional shade-enduring evergreen like this *Pinus montana* for accent, as at the Stroll Garden of the Hammond Museum in North Salem, New York. CHARLES MARDEN FITCH PHOTO

excavating except for individual trees or shrubs.) Nor do I believe in root pruning, which simply increases the ambition of a surface-rooter. Under my surface-rooting Norway and sugar maples where the soil was dry, hard, and meager, I made 8- to 10-inch pockets of rich, humusy soil between the thick roots and planted there the lovely blue spring phlox, *P. divaricata,* and the creeping, lavender-flowered evergreen myrtle. Here I fertilize heavily with a high-phosphorus material early in spring and lightly twice more during the growing season, knowing that the greedy surface roots will claim their tithe of all I provide. (See Color Section.) You will also find this to be true of other shaded areas—of lawn, of shrub borders, of the little gardens of annuals and perennials taking hold under your well-pruned trees. But there, with enough food and water, the proper kinds of plants will bloom as well as other kinds do in a sunny place.

If you have what appear to be hopeless areas, take a good look at the soil. You will probably find it heavily compacted, dry, perhaps with a greenish surface. Loosen it as deeply as strength permits with a spading fork, work in plenty of humus (commercial) or compost (homemade) or both, and, since the green is probably evidence of too much acidity, add also some horticultural lime—but not if you plan to grow azaleas and rhododendrons, for these prefer some acidity. In Chapter 6 you will find a formula for preparing soil for a woodland garden, and you can follow it for other areas, too.

Water Well

Too often it isn't shade that prevents flowers and grass under trees but absolute aridity, especially beneath big-leaved giants that hardly let a drop of rain come through. If the ground stays fearfully dry, even a flooding rain doesn't help because the water runs off instead of penetrating. Where soil is reasonably well prepared with plenty of compost or humus and then adequately fertilized, deep watering promotes growth that may actually be lush. Water deeply, especially in heavy shade. Keep alert for signs of drought and inadequate drainage.

A number of outdoor faucets and yards and yards of hose—to avoid wearisome dragging—make watering an easier task. An outlet on each side of the house is a great convenience and I fasten a removable metal rack beside it to hold a length of hose. (The rack hangs on a second set of screws in the cellar in winter to make hose storage convenient there.) New under-tree plantings are particularly in need of water the first two years or so and thereafter must not be neglected. Now I rarely have to water the great stretches of pachysandra under the balm-of-Gilead, which has no branches below 30 feet, but the phlox and myrtle on the brook slope under the surface-rooting maples need deep soaking almost every other week, especially through the usual summer weeks of drought, and no *light* sprinkling suffices there. Rather, it would be an encouragement to more enthusiastic surface-rooting, and then plants would deteriorate or die from dryness and heat.

To expect luxuriant budding on your fine shrubs in shade, your azaleas and rhododendrons, assure deep watering with a slow-running hose laid at the roots of each one and left there until you see actual puddling. I put the nozzle on a shingle or board to diffuse the stream; sometimes it takes an hour to do the job, sometimes half an hour, but attention all day long if you have many plants is usually in the cards.

For expanses of garden or groundcover, I like the fan sprinklers that rise up and bow low as they deliver the spray. They are a cooling sight for me on a hot day and are obviously welcomed by the plants. Those old-fashioned metal circles or squares that deliver water in a smaller radius are also useful. To reduce the loss by evaporation, keep the pressure low. Overhead sprinkling is, of course, more wasteful of water than ground application, but it's easier on *you* because you don't have to move a sprinkler as often as a hose nozzle.

Some years ago at the International Garden Show in Hamburg, Germany, a somewhat shaded section was delightfully patterned with a brick walk around areas of large stones and cement sections fitted with pipes of bubbling water to delight the birds. HERMANN NIESE PHOTO

It's a good plan, when you are involved in a big watering job through weeks of drought, to set sprinklers in place at night for their early-morning job. Then you can turn on faucets without having to wade through dew-wet grass. Do not be afraid of watering in full sunlight—it doesn't hurt the plants—or of evening waterings, unless you are located in a humid area where prolonged dampness exposes plants to bacterial attacks. Then 5 P.M. had better be your cut-off time, as it is mine.

Mulching

Mulch regularly with a material that will not pack tight. A 2-
to 3-inch mulch spread over your shaded plantings does wonders
for them by conserving moisture and keeping roots cool. It keeps
you cool too, for a well-mulched bed needs less watering. I have
used wood chips when I could get them, also chopped redwood
or pine bark. These break down slowly, permit good air and
water penetration, and are particularly nice-looking. I also use a
quantity of pine needles because I have them, and they also
make an attractive covering. They are slow to deteriorate and good
for the hollies and other broad-leaveds because of their acid re-
action, and they are not detrimental to the perennial borders where
I also spread them since I brush the needles aside every spring and
fertilize heavily there. Then I replace the mulch and usually add
to it as well.

Perhaps salt hay is readily available to you. It is good and
breaks down slowly, also it doesn't blow away like peanut and
cocoa hulls—which I tried only one year. Long ago I used peat
moss. At first it looked nice and later, worked into the soil, was
a good source of humus, but I found it caking so hard that water
ran off rather than through it, and strong wind always blew some
of it away, too. The lumpy kind stays put longer and lets some
water through, but even so, other kinds of mulch are better.

One year at the big horticultural exhibit "Planten un Blomen"
in Hamburg, Germany, I saw some brand-new types of mulch used
in quite stark gardens of contemporary style. Coarse gray charcoal
set off the sparse planting in one garden, small brown pieces of
cork in another, and coal in several others. The large dull chunks
were surprisingly pleasing, also the small shiny black pieces—such
imaginative uses of minerals with plants. And in this country
perhaps coal will become plentiful enough for gardens to get some
as well as furnaces. The coal certainly looked nice.

This chapter probably offers the most important advice I can give you based on my long experience with gardening in shade. I hope you will "read, mark, learn, and inwardly digest," as my English teacher used to urge us when assigning a difficult or important stretch of homework. Doubtless you agree with me that plants are far more interesting than practices. The trouble is that without these good procedures, you don't get very good plants.

Shade grasses flourish under high-pruned ash and sweetgum trees, and pachysandra grows under the heavy shade of a dogwood, *left*.

LAWNS, MOSS, AND PAVING

Crevice Plants for Small Spaces

Lawns in shade are a tricky business. For that matter, lawns in sun are too, and I think most of us get a lot more satisfaction out of our places if the lawn areas are kept to a minimum. True, a house is usually more attractively set off if there is *some* lawn but it doesn't have to be a tremendous sweep. Rather, we can depend on other means for good settings, particularly in shade.

Under deep-rooted, high-pruned trees, however, growing good grass is no more difficult in shade than in sun. A friend of mine, an especially practical and successful gardener, sows the same general grass mixture, plus one-fifth of clover, in her sunny lawn as in the shaded side stretch. She says she just lets the grasses fight it out according to preference and the survivors in both cases produce good green coverage.

Grass Seed for Shade

The average mixture, not the inexpensive kind with a lot of annual rye grass, usually includes a considerable amount of bluegrass and some fescues. The fescues that thrive in both sun and shade save the day in summer when bluegrass, unless constantly and heavily watered, tends to brown. In a predominantly shaded area (but not in the heavy shade of maples and some oaks), fescues alone give the best results. They are the most expensive of grass-seed mixtures, but if your lawn area is restricted, as mine certainly is, you will find fescues a good investment. Also, if you have some sunny stretches, the fescues will perform well there too. Examining labels, I have failed to find all-fescue mixtures locally, and please do read the labels before you buy. They list the types and percentages of the various grasses in the mixture. George W. Park Seed Co. offers a Dense Shade Formula "adapted to heavily shaded areas and will do well in lighter shade." It is made up mainly but not entirely of fescues. White Flower Farm offers a very fine Premium Mixture "of three fescues—Chewings, Creeping Red, and Pennlawn"—and the catalogue warns that this mixture will not do well in climates where nights remain hot. We do have *some* hot nights here but not enough to harm an all-fescue lawn. Burpee offers Shady Nook grass seed containing three excellent fescues and some fine-bladed perennial rye grass. (Addresses of these firms are given under Sources.)

And here I must admit to heresy, for I also add a fifth of clover to my lawn seed. Of course, clover is anathema to the purist, but clover thrives in shade, resists chinch bug and fungus attacks, and in humid conditions of weather or location is a real ally against bacterial diseases. In shade and humidity, as near a brook, bacterial disease is almost inevitable. Some yellow spots usually develop here in July. Fall seeding and fertilizing allow me to treat these as a temporary condition, but spraying with benomyl (Benlate)

In the dense shade of an enormous sycamore-maple a terrace of flagstones set in cement takes the place of grass for most of the area. Pots of pink tuberous begonias and lavender fuchsias in hanging baskets suspended on the fence and a camellia in a redwood tub bring color to this little garden. Ferns and wildflowers grow in the raised bed. GEORGE TALOUMIS PHOTO

when your own discomfort is acute or the thermometer and hygrometer together register degrees adding up to 150 is certainly a safer procedure. Furthermore, agronomists continue to work for greater disease resistance in all types of grass. (If you sow clover and later apply a weed-killer, which you shouldn't have to do in the shade with proper seeding and fertilizer, be sure the preparation is not also a clover-killer.) On the following pages are my suggestions based on my own schedule for my limited areas of lawn in shade.

White pebbles spread under
a crab-apple tree are a good
substitute for grass in a
difficult area. Woodbine
covers a fence at the left.
GEORGE TALOUMIS PHOTO

Lawn Schedule

March–April. On a still day rake up the winter accumulation if
the lawn is dry enough. A shaded lawn stays wet longer than a
lawn in sun, so act accordingly. Scratch bare spots—don't dig up
a lot in spring—and seed there but not the whole lawn. (Wait till
fall for this.) About March 15 (but wait till April if lawn is
still sloppy wet), apply a high-nitrogen, slow-release organic fertilizer as 10–6–4, 12–4–8, or 15–8–12 according to package directions;
a spreader is helpful if the area to be covered is extensive. I
don't use a roller on a shaded lawn. I apply lime only if a soil
test indicates the need in areas I suspect are highly acid.

May. Start mowing with blades at 2 inches (2½ to 3 inches
for fescues alone). Let short clippings fall (they are good mulching

material); use a catcher or rake up clippings if they are long and showing a heavy build-up. Then they encourage fungus trouble. In dry weather, now and later, water enough to give your lawn one inch of moisture a week, perhaps more if weather is hot, say, above 70 degrees. Put a can under the outside drip of the lawn sprinkler so that you can measure the amount. It may take hours to do a good job but avoid watering a shaded lawn after dark, and avoid overwatering. Too much water and slow drying, as in shade, also invite fungus attacks. Early morning is a good time.

Summer. In hot dry weather, skip mowing unless you have watered so much that the grass is green and overlong. Don't let your mowing service, if you have one, con you into a weekly job when a weekly job is bad for your lawn. In cool weather, I often scatter a little extra fertilizer close to tree trunks for encouragement to the grass there.

September. For me, this is really Lawn Month insofar as any month can be so designated here. As nights grow longer, days cooler, and fall rains start, conditions are ideal for lawn care. Then I again tend to any bad spots and also apply high-nitrogen, slow-release fertilizer over the whole area, using about twice the spring amount. If the whole lawn area looks meager, I do an all-over seeding.

October. Keep raking. Soggy leaves collecting on a shaded lawn spell disaster. Decide on a spot or two for a concave compost pile and dump the leaves there. The hollow center catches the rain, which speeds decay.

Flagstones, Moss, and Crevice Plants

In dense shade under beeches, *most* maples, *low-branched* oaks, and catalpas, I think it is foolish to struggle for grass. Why not spread stones under a big tree or set brick or flagstones there for a terrace with some pretty little creepers in between? Attractive crevice plants are listed in the chart at the end of the chapter. With

A brick terrace on two
levels makes a delightful
outdoor room for living
and dining under a
high- and open-pruned
silk-tree, *Albizzia julibrissin*.
A stretch of woodland on
the south protects the
terrace from the hot
summer sun. GEORGE
TALOUMIS PHOTO

a pleasing arrangement you can have a comfortable carefree outdoor sitting room, instead of an ailing, demanding area that by courtesy only can be called a lawn.

Or, have you thought of moss? Moss grew spontaneously between the stepping stones on the brook bank, and I was so grateful. Wherever a little patch of moss could be spared for a bare spot, I lifted it and carefully reset it until I had good coverage. I forbid mowing and avoided fertilizer there where the self-sufficient moss was thriving.

Now, where to get moss? Except on the West Coast, we do not go in for moss gardens, so charming in their varying velvet greenness there, and kept so by misting. The woods are, of course, one source, and maybe you can lift good sheets of moss from logs, boulders, or right from the forest floor. One man who does this is making a charming moss garden. Since commercial sources of moss in sufficient quantity do not exist in the East, here we must depend on spontaneous appearance or collecting from the woods.

CREVICE PLANTS FOR SHADED WALKS AND TERRACES

Most paving plants flourish with half, not deep, shade. Moss is more useful for deep shade; I gather it wherever it grows here and tuck it in between paving stones above the brook bank. If flagstones are sunk a little, grass, especially fescues, will thrive around them and can be conveniently mowed along with the lawn.

Name	Height in Inches	Description	Culture
Ajuga reptans Bugleweed	3–4	Glossy foliage, blue, purple, or white flowers; May–June.	Light to deep shade; also a good groundcover.
Arenaria verna caespitosa Moss Sandwort	1–2	Tiny white flowers in May; mossy foliage. Has been called the perfect paving plant.	Half-shade; gritty soil with plenty of sand.
Asperula odorata Sweet Woodruff	6–8	White, May–June flowers, whorled leaves, attractive all summer.	Partial shade; a darling plant. Also an excellent groundcover.
Bluets, see *Houstonia*			
Bugleweed, see *Ajuga*			

Creeping Charlie, Jennie, see *Lysimachia*			
Gill-over-the-ground, Ground-ivy, see *Nepeta*			
Houstonia serpyllifolia Creeping Bluets	creeper	Delightful mats of growth, tiny, enamel-like, deep-blue May flowers, native.	Flourishes in pockets of sand, peat moss, and loam mixed; light shade and moisture.
London Pride, see *Saxifraga*			
Lysimachia nummularia Moneywort, Creeping Charlie or Jennie	creeper	Rounded leaves, yellow June–July flowers.	Energetic in any soil in shade or sun; it got out of hand for me in the lawn but I liked it for difficult areas across the brook. It is an excellent pavement plant.
Mazus reptans	1–2	Lavender flowers, June–July. Does well in city gardens.	Light shade, fast stem-rooting creeper, a pest in lawns. Good between *shaded* flag-stones; stands some walking on; not always cold-hardy.
Mentha requienii Creeping Mint	creeper	Tiny lavender flowers in whorls, July–Aug.; typical square mint stems.	Shade or sun, fast spreader by underground stems; nice mint odor when trod upon between flagstones.

Name	Height in Inches	Description	Culture
Mint, see *Mentha*			
Moneywort, see *Lysimachia*			
Moss Sandwort, see *Arenaria*			
Nepeta hederacea Ground-ivy, Gill-over-the-ground	creeper	Blue spring-and-summer whorls of flowers, native.	Light to full shade or sun, preferably in moist soil; watch to avoid an unwanted takeover.
Pearlwort, see *Sagina*			
Phlox stolonifera Creeping Phlox	8	Forms mats; clusters of lavender flowers in spring, native and hardy.	Light shade, also thrives in open woodland.
Sagina subulata Pearlwort	4	Evergreen mossy growth; blooms July–Aug.	Excellent between very shaded stepping stones.
Saxifraga umbrosa London Pride, Saxifrage	10	Leathery mounding rosettes, pink or white spring flowers in airy sprays.	Prefers rocky limestone soil. Half-shade fine for this one.

Sedum acre Goldmoss Stonecrop	2	Creeper with tiny yellow summer flowers, curly tufts of leaves.	Any soil rather dry; light shade.
album	8	Large evergreen mats, flat panicles of white flowers in profusion.	
Speedwell, see *Veronica*			
Sweet Woodruff, see *Asperula*			
Veronica prostrata (*rupestris*) Speedwell	8	Tufted growth; pale-blue flowers, May–June.	A reliable spreader between stones in half-shade; avoid the terrible lawn weed *V. filiformis*.

Four charming groundcovers pictured here and on the following pages. Shown above, the rose-pink fringed bleedingheart with ferny foliage, *Dicentra eximia,* blooms spring to fall. GEORGE TALOUMIS PHOTO

GROUNDCOVERS
THE SHADE GARDENER'S FRIEND

Common and Uncommon Kinds

When it comes down to it, all land plants are groundcovers, but for our own small purposes we select low-growing spreading plants, evergreen or deciduous, annual or perennial, even certain bulbs, that will cover shaded areas attractively and undemandingly. Great sweeps of one kind can certainly be dramatic, as we see in public places, and from these we can adapt ideas to our own less spectacular needs.

Recently at the great "Planten un Blomen" show in Hamburg, Germany, I saw glorious sweeps of the annual impatiens, white, pink, and salmon in separate colors, but such a glorious panorama required the gardener I didn't have, so I could admire but not copy. Then I saw a stand of the charming fringed bleedingheart, *Dicentra eximia,* making clumps of ferny foliage in light shade. Even in late September there was bloom, and I knew that this

White foamflower, *Tiarella cordifolia*, for April to July. GEORGE TALOUMIS PHOTO

had continued from spring when the nodding, heart-shaped, rosy flowers would have opened in profusion. Although this plant was familiar to me, as a groundcover it was new and just right for a fairly moist location.

I saw also the ineffable blue Jacobs-ladder, *Polemonium reptans,* long a favorite, but I had never seen it so widely planted; it was, of course, in second bloom for its lavish spring display always has to be cut back, and I had a feeling there must have been some dull weeks here while the plant renewed itself. (*P. caeruleum* cultivars are taller and fine for perennial borders.)

Then at Kew Gardens outside London, I admired drifts of the lavender autumn-crocus, *Colchicum,* set as a groundcover under

Sweet woodruff, *Asperula
odorata,* for May to
mid-June, is also a
charming crevice plant.
GEORGE TALOUMIS PHOTO

Early spring-blooming white violets for light open shade are one of my indispensables, here in a broad sweep interplanted with Christmas ferns for later effect. CHARLES MARDEN FITCH PHOTO

Daphne mezereum. This was the first time I ever liked the autumn-crocus, for the flowers always appeared naked and shivering to me. But now I realized that closely planted it could bring a sheet of fall color to a shrub planting, of forsythia, for instance, but hardly under a stretch of daphne, as, here, since a precarious plant or two of this shrub is all that has ever survived for me. A label indicated that grape-hyacinths set among the colchicums brought under-neath color there in spring. Well, I thought, bulbs as groundcovers for shrubs; I had never used them so. Thinking about it, I realized my own use of groundcovers while comforting could perhaps be more imaginative.

Anyway, I have enjoyed the tremendous spreads of ubiquitous evergreen pachysandra that flourish under the trees and shrubs

English ivy makes a superb green cover under trees; it must not be exposed to winter sun, for it may brown without snow cover.
GEORGE TALOUMIS PHOTO

The vining myrtle, *Vinca minor,* here covers a steep bank beside a flight of steps.
GEORGE TALOUMIS PHOTO

A great bed of pachysandra makes an all-season green covering for an otherwise barren area under a low-branched, surface-rooting beech tree. GEORGE TALOUMIS PHOTO

along the right side of the contracted front lawn, balancing my driveway bed on the left. Some day this area, too, might be put to pachysandra if the shaded garden of shrubs and perennials there proves too taxing. I have also depended on broad sweeps of pachysandra along the path to the Round Garden.

English ivy has beautifully solved a grass problem in the deep shade of the arbor beside the house, and it has also filled in dark unlikely spots next to the house, where judicious pruning protects foundations and house walls from the depredations of this exuberant vine.

The evergreen myrtle is another dependable groundcover here. *With due attention* to food and water, it even thrives under maples, and I feel a certain gratitude to this plant that made beautiful a real problem area in deep shade.

Elsewhere lily-of-the-valley and white violets make lovely patches, and beside the big planting of ferns little colonies of foamflower and bluets are charming. Across the brook, yellow-flowering epimedium shines out, and below the big rock I see the white sweet woodruff.

Don't feel distressed, please, if your shaded areas are extensive and heretofore have been unmanageable. You can readily settle for the indispensable pachysandra, ivy, and myrtle, or be more imaginative in some areas. You might even forego under-tree plants, and instead level off deeply shaded areas, set flagstones with crevice plants between or settle for a surface of small stones. I like chunky white quartz for this purpose spread in a regular or free-form pattern around a tree trunk. But if it's plants you prefer, look at the possibilities in the chart that follows. I really dote on these various groundcovers that have so gracefully eased my own gardening life.

GROUNDCOVERS FOR THE SHADE

Less lawn, more groundcover makes for easier gardening, particularly in shade. See also the charts of Crevice Plants at the end of Chapter 3 and of Ferns following Chapter 6.

(E=Evergreen; D=Deciduous)

Name	Height in Inches	E or D	Foliage, Fruit, Flowers	Culture	Remarks
Ajuga reptans Bugleweed	3–4	E or Semi	Purple, blue, white flowers May–June, glossy foliage.	Light to deep shade.	Fast useful spreader. Also with variegated leaves (not my favorite).
Aegopodium podograria Goutweed	12–14	D	White flowers in June.	Full shade, naturalized here, unfortunately.	Terrible invader; plant this only in a desperate situation. Otherwise beware!
Asarum, see Woodland Chart Ginger					
Asperula odorata Sweet Woodruff	6–8	D	White May–June flowers; leaves used in May wine.	Moist shaded areas, here under rock ledge.	Charming leaves in whorled tiers; small bulbs can grow amid foliage.

Bugleweed, see *Ajuga*

Ceratostigma plumbaginoides Plumbago	6–10	D	Deep-blue flowers Aug.–Sept.; glossy green tufts of leaves turn bronze in fall.	Light shade.	Spring growth starts late, plants spread rapidly, can become a weed. Good in city garden.
Chrysogonum virginianum Goldenstar	6–10	D	Yellow flowers Apr.–June, native.	Partial shade, rich, moist soil.	Not reliably hardy, worth chancing for lovely, long golden bloom.
Convallaria majalis Lily-of-the-valley	8	D	White, very fragrant flowers May–June, native.	Open shade to partial sun; in deep shade no bloom.	I simply remove tops in early fall if spider mites attack; needs heavy fertilizing and much water.
Cotoneaster adpressa Creeping Cotoneaster	prostrate	D	All valued for red fruits. Leaves turn beet-red in fall.	Light shade.	Very slow-growing; dwarf 'Praecox' is faster.
dammeri Bearberry Cotoneaster	12	E	Effective white flowers.		May root along stems; good cover for banks.

Name	Height in Inches	E or D	Foliage, Fruit, Flowers	Culture	Remarks
Cotoneaster continued *horizontalis* Rockspray	36	E or Semi	Tall flat-branch-ing shrub.		*C. apiculata*, cranberry cotoneaster, with longer berries. Both good on slopes.
Dead Nettle, see *Lamium*					
Dicentra eximia Fringed Bleedingheart	12–15	D	Rose-pink spring display, some repetition through fall, native.	Partial-shade and moisture.	Grows in clumps; fine ferny foliage. I have seen magnificent spreads of this.
English Ivy, see *Hedera*					
Epimedium alpinum rubrum	6–9	D	Red Apr.–May flowers.	Tolerates deep shade, rich acid soil.	Choice, this small epimedium almost un-known, an excellent groundcover for wild gardens.
macranthum niveum	9	D	Long-spurred white flowers, handsome leaves.		Aristocratic beauty.

	8–12	D	Yellow flowers.	Shade or sun.	Showy, pretty associated with rocks.
pinnatum	8–12	D	Yellow flowers.		Showy, pretty associated with rocks.
Euonymus fortunei (*radicans*) Wintercreeper	prostrate	E	Leaf shape varies.	Shade or sun.	Rambling for banks, purple winter tones. 'Coloratus' among best for groundcover.
Ferns, see Woodland Chart					
Foamflower, see *Tiarella*					
Forget-me-not, see *Myosotis*					
Galax aphylla, see Woodland Chart					
Gaultheria procumbens Wintergreen	trailing	E	White May–June bellflowers, red fall-winter berries, native.	Light to deep shade, rich acid soil.	Good groundcover, prospers under pine trees.
Goldenstar, see *Chrysogonum*					
Goutweed, see *Aegopodium*					

Name	Height in Inches	E or D	Foliage, Fruit, Flowers	Culture	Remarks
Hedera helix English ivy	6	E	Glossy dark-green leaves.	Light or deep shade.	Avoid winter sun; keep away from house foundation; climber or trailer.
baltica			Small-leaved.		Hardier than type; both spread fast.
Jacobs-ladder, see *Polemonium reptans*					
Japanese Spurge, see *Pachysandra*					
Lamium maculatum Dead Nettle	6–8	Semi-E	Lavender or white Apr.–Aug. flowers, ascending stems. Green or green-and-silver foliage, native.	Light shade.	Indestructible, invasive but fast useful spreader; prune off unattractive flowers.
Lilyturf, see *Liriope*					
Lily-of-the-valley, see *Convallaria*					

Liriope muscari Lilyturf	12–24	E	Lilac or white, flowers Aug.–Oct.; grassy foliage.	Light shade, good in South.	Needs sheltered area, may not be hardy north of New York City.
Lysimachia nummularia, see Crevice Plants Creeping Charlie or Jenny					
Memorial Rose, see *Rosa*					
Myosotis scorpioides (*palustris*) Forget-me-not	12–20	D	Yellow-eyed blue flowers, a few pink, Apr.–Sept.	Half-shade, self-sows freely.	Nice beside brook or pool, in marsh. Lovely bedding plant under my apple tree; also charming in woodland.
Myrtle, see *Vinca*					
Pachysandra terminalis Japanese Spurge	8–12	E	Tiny white flowers, May, dark-green foliage.	Shade to shifting sunlight, any soil.	Fast grower; takes hold quickly if new plantings are watered.
Parthenocissus quinquefolia, see Vine Chart					

Name	Height in Inches	E or D	Foliage, Fruit Flowers	Culture	Remarks
Paxistima canbyi	12	E	Prostrate shrub, native.	Light shade, acid soil.	Spreads slowly, best for limited area.
Periwinkle, see *Vinca*					
Phlox divaricata canadensis Blue Phlox	8–12	D	Lavender or white Apr.–May flowering, lovely, native.	Light shade or sun, border or rock garden; indispensable.	Exquisite, spreads quickly if planted in rich soil, watered, fed well; tolerates surface maple roots here. Bulbs will grow among clumps.
stolonifera Creeping Blue Phlox	8	D	Forms mats; clusters of lavender flowers in spring, native.	Light shade.	'Blue Ridge' and 'Lavender Lady' good; also thrives in open woodland.
Polemonium reptans Jacobs-ladder	12	D	Blue flowers, May–June, native.	Light to fairly deep shade, rich moist soil.	Fine ferny foliage, good concealer for bulbs; dies down, then renews, repeats bloom.

Rosa wichuraiana Memorial Rose	trailing	Semi-E	White flowers, late summer.	Light shade or full light, not deep shade.	Dependable for banks and slopes, roots where it touches.
'Max Graf'			Single pink.		
Sweet Woodruff, see *Asperula*					
Tiarella, see Woodland Chart Foamflower					
Veronica officinalis Common Speedwell	creeper	Semi-E	Pale blue, May–July flowers, native.	Shade of any degree	Fine low spreader, not a refined grower.
Vinca minor Myrtle, Periwinkle	trailing	E	Lavender or white, Apr.–May flowers. 'Bowles Variety' larger deeper flowers.	Light to quite deep shade but less bloom there.	Colorful and effective, spreads fairly fast if watered well and fed until established.
Viola, see Woodland Chart Violet					
Wintercreeper, see *Euonymus*					

A shaded border around a greening lawn blooms white and yellow in spring before trees are in full leaf. Against a background of burgeoning forsythia bushes, a long border of early Kaufmanniana tulips 'Fair Lady', white hyacinths 'Carnegie', pink hyacinths 'Anne Marie', and daffodils 'Flower Carpet' is a glorious sight, with the fragrance of the hyacinths a pleasant extra. PHOTO BY MALAK

5

A WEALTH OF BLOOM
FROM SPRING AND SUMMER BULBS
Most Rewarding of All Shade Plants

March and April are delectable months for the shade gardener with all the lovely early-blooming bulbs adrift with color, the blues more prevalent now than at almost any other time in the gardening year. Under the leafless limbs of apple tree, silverbell, fringetree, and tall lilacs, colonies of bulbs open flowers that are appreciated all the more because they come first and there is little competition with other blooming plants. Here late in March and early April only the Cornelian-cherry, the vernal witch-hazel, and the airy spicebush are in bloom above them. Earlier the stark look of winter still holds, but aconites, crocuses, snowdrops, scillas, and the species tulips dance in the cold breezes and sparkle in the bleak sunshine. I think the early bulbs, wildflowers, and ferns (of the next chapter) are probably the most rewarding of all shade plants; certainly the early bulbs make no demands even for light in summer, their foliage ripening before trees are in heavy leaf. (See Color Section.)

In February (sometimes in late January) and some two weeks

before the earliest crocuses, winter-aconites, *Eranthis hyemalis,* offer great patches of golden bloom to lighten dreary winter days. I do urge you to plant this choice and little-known winter bulb. Visitors here are charmed by it; yet it is neither rare nor difficult, and it seeds and spreads mightily. In the cold sunlight in a southern exposure under the warm walls of the living room, it is a cheerful sight, the buttercup blooms small but effective.

The winter-aconites, 5 to 6 inches high, come from tubers that are set out just as soon as you get them late in August or early September, and please not less than twenty-five tubers, and fifty will please you much more. Soak them overnight before planting them 2 inches deep and 3 inches apart. Keep them well watered the first autumn, thereafter you need not bother. As the later crocuses, scillas, and chionodoxas take over, flowers of the aconites fade while each tuber produces its own lacy green parasol, which lasts for some six weeks or more. My aconite colonies have prospered and the flowers have opened earliest in places close to sun-warmed house walls, a little later under the birches and shrubs beside the driveway. In a rock garden with a southern slope or woodland, or carpeting your shrub border, aconites will delight you. Fortunately, they prefer shade as they ripen and disappear after bloom.

About this same time *Narcissus minimus,* a doll-size daffodil only 3 inches tall, blooms ahead of all its tribe, and requires the near view. I plant it at the front step where its yellow gleam surprises me every February.

The nodding snowdrops also open now, sometimes even while patches of snow linger beside them to confirm their name. The "giant" snowdrop, *Galanthus elwesii,* to 8 inches, comes first, "bold and assured in the face of winter storm and stress," as Louise Beebe Wilder put it. For woodland plantings *G. nivalis* has a less formal air, and, of course, I mean the single forms. I don't really like the doubles. One place not to plant any of them is in a pachysandra bed. They just can't compete; all you get for years to come, unless you find time to dig them out, is weedy foliage, no flowers. However, snowdrops will thrive and bloom merrily in a lightly shaded bed of myrtle.

Crocuses and Others

The species crocuses appear with the aconites and snowdrops or soon after. If you are acquainted only with the big Dutch hybrids, do get to know these earlier 3- to 6-inch little fellows. They are enchanting, opening small but sturdy yellow, purple, or lavender cups in the cold winter air. The species *C. chrysanthus, C. sieberi,* and *tomasinianus* are grand colonizers, and the varieties —'Blue Bird', 'Cream Beauty', and the double 'Goldilocks'—most attractive. All look nice planted in mixture, not in the lawn though, where crocuses look spotty and are a great nuisance if mowing is to wait upon their maturing.

The Dutch hybrids, taller and showier, have more of a garden look, and I would not use these in woodland. Here double lines of my favorite white, purple-lined 'Pickwick' edge the front flagstone walk and groups of the white orange-anthered 'Peter Pan' and 'Yellow Mammoth' brighten beds beneath east windows. I see I planted a few leftovers along the drive, where they are showy even in the midst of pachysandra, but such an arrangement is unworthy of them. Certainly autumn efforts pay off when you see your crocuses in spring bloom.

And perhaps with them you can have the purple winter iris, the bulbous *I. reticulata.* I always see its grassy growth under the kitchen casements by mid-February but the flowers don't make an appearance every year.

Early in March the trout-lilies or dogtooth-violets, *Erythronium,* put on a modest but extensive performance near the brook. These really must be naturalized for they don't take to formal garden life. They volunteered here, and if the spring is cold and wet, I almost miss them for it is a damp walk to their habitat and their appearance is brief, about ten days. If you have woodland with light shade, do plant these engaging small lilies of turkscap form.

Yellow winter aconites,
Eranthis hyemalis. PHOTO
BY MALAK

Yellow trout-lilies,
Erythronium are among the
earliest. PHOTO BY MALAK

Yellow petticoat narcissus, *N. bulbocodium*. PHOTO BY MALAK

Yellow Kaufmanniana tulip 'Mendelssohn' with a rose heart open soon after. PHOTO BY MALAK

Mine came yellow but you could have white, pink, or lavender if you prefer and they are charming in mixture.

Warm spells in March produce a blue-and-white mosaic under the fringetree at the front steps. Here the blue-lined, white lemon-squill, *Puschkinia scilloides,* offers a lovely mignonette fragrance, though you have to go practically prone to catch it. The blue-and-white glory-of-the-snow, *Chionodoxa,* blooms with it; the intensely blue 6-inch Siberian squill, *Scilla sibirica,* 'Spring Beauty', gives vibrancy to the picture. But so strong is the blue of the scillas that you need not plant them near the house as I have. A big patch under a tree makes an effective picture even from a distance, and these hardy bulbs multiply wonderfully. For golden accent to pick up the blues, I add a few bulbs of the intrepid 'February Gold' narcissus. None of these little ones need thoughtful planning; just use a quantity of each. Here they combine beautifully behind the myrtle edging of the walk.

Weeks after *Scilla sibirica* has declared for rest, the Spanish bluebells or wood-hyacinths, *S. hispanica (campanulata)*, white and lavender, are a lovely sight along the grass path of the Fern Garden. The mounds of green send up strong 12- to 15-inch spikes of bloom and these are set off by the pink-lavender clouds of wild geranium. Starting in late April this pretty picture lasts for about a month. Probably there is no better garden investment than wood-hyacinths, and you might want some pinks as well as blues and whites, for this is a bulb that is lovely in mixture. My original twenty-five now number hundreds, maybe thousands, for I have shared the largess with friends, and also used them as bedding in the Round Garden where the summer shade is really deep.

Equally long-lived and blooming about the same time is the spring snowflake, *Leucojum vernum,* with white, green-tipped bells on 10-inch sprays. Not brilliantly effective like the wood-hyacinths, the snowflakes are an interesting addition to the list of pretty, small bulbs to grow in shade.

Above, left. The purple-striped white 'Pickwick' crocus; *right*, tiny gray-blue *Puschinia. Below, left.* Grape-hyacinths, *Muscari*, in shades of blue and white; *right*, snowdrops, *Galanthus*, brighten shaded gardens in February and March. PHOTOS BY MALAK

Hyacinths—True and False

When it comes to hyacinths, I'd like to have all this printed in bold type. Hyacinths are among my favorites but how few of you seem to plant them. Really, you don't know what you are missing. In a northern exposure, against the house and next to the back door, the richly scented light-blue 'Myosotis' and white 'Innocence' make even a trip to the garbage box a pleasure. Perhaps you will prefer the lovely 'Pink Pearl' or 'King of the Blues' but with this set some whites, for the dark king appears gloomy by himself.

I think hyacinths look nice in rows as well as in colonies, and I set the bulbs 8 to 10 inches deep, so the heavy heads won't flop over in the rain, and about 8 inches apart. This leaves space for the insertion of small in-bud annual plants to grow while the hyacinths take their time about maturing in May. I must mention also the yellow hyacinth, 'City of Haarlem'. What a handsome one this is. For three years I enjoyed it along a walk and as edging to an azalea bed but then it dwindled, some bulbs setting no blooms, others smaller ones, for I had not taken into account that English ivy roots in one location and pachysandra in another would gradually win the competition. Hyacinths get the garden off to early color in April and, depending on weather, will last through most of the month. Be sure to plant enough to have extras for cutting. They last well indoors and scent a room deliciously.

Grape-hyacinths are not true hyacinths but *Muscari*. They look like small upside-down bunches of grapes and smell rather like the Concords. 'Heavenly Blue' is the one I have. It blooms about mid-April, disappears, and then sends up winter-hardy grassy foliage in September. I have one big patch of it along the brook steps under a maple tree and another as groundcover for tree peonies under the hawthorn tree.

I marvel at the endurance of these early-flowering bulbs. One year my diary recorded snow on April 8; 26 degrees on April 9; driving rain April 10 (it was a wretched watery spring) ; then several days at 32 degrees, followed by heat at 50 degrees. Yet there was complete recovery of hyacinths and daffodils by afternoon. Some of the scillas, having been longer in bloom, still looked rather floppy.

I must add a word here about the wild star-of-Bethlehem, *Ornithogalum umbellatum,* big clumps of which I have been pleased to welcome even in the cultivated beds. From dark grassy clumps, rise white, green-striped, starlike flowers late in May, delightful though uninvited. These just could become a nuisance for they are vigorous and spreading, but plants are easily lifted for sharing with friends or transplanting to the woods. Here in summer they are in really deep shade.

Tulips

If you know only the big sun-demanding tulips of May, it is time you discovered the quite different and less spectacular species (botanical tulips) of April. Some, like *Tulipa violacea,* bloom very early so you might enjoy this purple with such species crocus as the yellow *C. chrysanthus* and silver-lavender *C. tomasinianus.* A pleasing April parade might start with the water lily tulip, *T. kaufmanniana,* ivory white with carmine-tinted outer petals—or one of its charming variations like my favorite apricot 'Fritz Kreisler' or yellow 'Mendelssohn'—and proceed with *T. fosteriana* 'Yellow Empress', and some brilliant Greigii hybrids, which bloom so well for me with hyacinths under the leafless Christmas-berry-tree, where, later, summer shade is deep.

I hope you won't miss the endearing red-and-white-striped lady tulip, *T. clusiana,* about 8 inches high. It holds its own against April storms and makes a stalwart line under the wisteria-draped arbor where summer sun never penetrates. You might also like a little patriotic April scene like mine, featuring the 10-inch vermilion, cluster-flowered *T. praestans* 'Fusilier', deep-blue scillas, and white hyacinths. Under an open-pruned, still leafless crab-apple tree beside the driveway, these make an amusing picture. Perhaps you will have a spot in your rock garden for such a grouping.

If you have never grown these species tulips, you might start with a mixture of them. This will be full of surprises and nice for April when fewer garden flowers vie for attention. In light shade you can also enjoy in April the single and double tulips listed as Early. They aren't as spectacular as the taller May-flowering Darwin, Cottage, and Parrot tulips, which must have sun, although the yellow-flushed, red-veined Darwin 'Gudoshnik' has prospered for me just at the edge of apple-tree shade. The single earlies have done well on the south side of the long driveway bed. (I've never grown the double earlies because I don't really like them.) Good single earlies include the pure white 'Diana', rose 'Proserpine', yellow 'Mon Tresor', and spectacular, scented, orange-scarlet 'De Wet', all growing about a foot high. I think shade gardeners can get a lot more mileage out of tulips than is commonly supposed; we just need to experiment more. Maybe those May beauties are not so sun-demanding as we have been led to believe.

Narcissus (Daffodils)

For open-shade plantings, you will be wise to select early varieties of narcissus as with tulips. Daffodils need to ripen their foliage in full light which dims as trees leaf out. It is, of course, much too dark under broadleaf evergreens and coniferous trees; indeed, bulbs set out there would be unlikely to survive.

My own plantings beneath the apple tree, on the rocky slope under giant oaks, and in the shaded Fern Garden have lasted for years. What is important beside full light early in spring, is freedom from the root competition of thick groundcovers or surface-rooting trees. Under trees I have been careful to fertilize heavily after flowering while bulbs are developing next year's embryo blossoms. I like to use a soluble plant food, and near the house I apply this from a watering can, the "rose" removed.

In the shadow of a spruce tree, yellow daffodils, 'Tunis' and 'Flower Carpet', with the early Darwin tulip 'Gudoshnik', well fertilized after flowering, bloom brilliantly year after year. PHOTO BY MALAK

Groundcovers that bulbs can live with here include, among others, sweet woodruff, *Asperula odorata;* foamflower, *Tiarella cordifolia;* and violets. When the yellow-cupped white 'Laurens Koster' narcissus opens in April above purple and white violets, it is a pretty sight indeed. Where daffodils are next to English ivy, I keep after the vine so that it does not encroach, and I have now transplanted the bulbs I had hoped would thrive in very shaded plantings of myrtle. In more open myrtle beds, there is no problem, nor in colonies among Christmas ferns, and this is a good combination, for the new fern growth, to a degree, conceals the maturing bulb foliage, a necessary but never an engaging aspect of bulb plantings.

In the years I have been gardening at Stony Brook Cottage, I have enjoyed many daffodils from miniatures to taller all-gold and all-white varieties, and the Poetaz types with a sweet scent. Here are some favorites that have bloomed well for me:

'Cheerfulness'	'Geranium'
'Cragford'	'King Alfred'
'Dick Wellband'	'Mrs. E. H. Krelage'
'Duke of Windsor'	'Mt. Hood'
'February Gold'	'Thalia'

'White Lady', a very old one, probably old Pheasant's Eye, *N. poeticus,* is everywhere here for I have been digging up and distributing clumps about the place for years. As a rule, trumpet daffodils follow grape-hyacinths and open before the early tulips and Dutch hyacinths.

My diaries indicate no failures among these, only some preferences, as white in association with the brook and pure yellows for the far view, but do select your own early varieties from well-illustrated catalogues. The possibilities are delirious!

If you will take care to plant where winter and early-spring light is strong, in enriched soil (moderately rootfree), and fertilize yearly, I feel sure you can enjoy daffodils for many years, as I have. Special packaged fertilizers for bulbs are available and fine, but superphosphate or bonemeal with unleached wood ashes saved from the fireplace are what I use. Catalogues offer a tremendous choice of narcissus types and color variations, though I would not recommend pinks for shade or the reversed bicolors. Bear in mind that narcissus flowers turn toward the sun, and in certain locations this could prevent their looking toward you as you wish.

If you are planting in a border or garden, and not in drifts as I mostly do, you will get good effects and be less tempted to remove maturing foliage before you should if you place your daffodils behind late-appearing perennials. Chrysanthemums and fall asters, astilbes, balloon-flowers, and daylilies won't conceal the early blooms but will do much to 'hide floppy foliage. You don't really have to wait until it turns yellow. I never do.

BULBS FOR SUMMER

Lilies

Among lilies for shade, you have a fairly wide choice. For mid to late June, there is the white madonna lily, *Lilium candidum,* which blooms well in a light open situation in soil mixed with lime and wood ashes. Plant it shallow with only an inch or so of covering, and in August or as soon thereafter as you can get the bulbs. Keep the site damp for the first autumn. *L. hansonii,* also for June, is orange-yellow, a fragrant Japanese lily. It needs deep planting. In the wild garden the waxy white clusters of *L. martagon album* look lovely this month. Plant bulb 3 to 4 inches deep. It is prettier than the typical purple-pink form, which has an unpleasant odor.

The golden 'Joan Evans', a Mid-Century Hybrid, for late June on, not only tolerates shade here but flourishes and propagates in conditions that cannot even be called "open." In June–July, the apricot-to-yellow Nankeen lily with a pink flush grows in half-shade and is not particular about soil.

In midsummer three hardy natives do well in light-to-medium

In summer, pink speciosum
lilies bloom year after year
here in midday shade with
an evergreen background.
GEORGE TALOUMIS PHOTO

shade. *L. canadense,* the meadow lily, produces yellow to pale
orange down-facing flowers on 5-foot stalks. The American turkscap lily, *L. superbum,* is a deeper color, orange to red, and the
flowers are quite open. At this season, too, the wood lily, *L.
philadelphicum,* with orange spotted-purple upward-facing flowers, often grows at the edge of woodland. This one is planted about
3 inches deep, the other two, deeper.

Later, August into September, two 3- to 4-foot vigorous beauties,
L. speciosum album, 'White Champion', and the "true pink lily,"
L. s. rubrum, have proved indestructible even when crowded and
shaded by encroaching shrubs. Cover these stem rooters with about
6 inches of soil.

Be sure your lilies have good drainage; raise the beds if there
is any doubt, for these bulbs tolerate shade but not standing
water.

Tuberous Begonias and Caladiums

You could enjoy many more than two of the handsome, summer-blooming, tender bulbs if you wish, but more than two require more effort than I care to expend in view of a multitude of other garden commitments. Today I let the florist start my two—tuberous begonias and caladiums—though actually they are easy do-it-yourself plants.

Tuberous begonias are extraordinarily handsome as bedding or hanging basket plants. They come in various colors—white, pink, red, yellow, and orange—and in various forms—double, rose, picotee, and multiflora, these having small but many flowers. I saw one particularly handsome bed of crimson tuberous begonias interspersed with fragrant purple heliotrope.

Instead of direct planting, you can get the effect of bedding by setting groups of potted plants under a tree on top of the soil. This type of begonia does unusually well in pots and produces extra-large flowers. If you prefer direct planting, set the tubers, preferably of 2- to 2-½-inch diameter, half an inch deep, always hollow side up, in well-drained humusy soil with some sand. Work in a little organic fertilizer beforehand. Most important is an open, airy, but not windy, location of shifting light. A couple of hours of morning or afternoon sunshine are fine, but not more. Except in cool climates begonias perish in full sun, and they bloom sparsely, if at all, in deep shade where they are so often mistakenly planted. A 2-inch mulch of wood chips or dehydrated cow manure (this also has fertility) improves propects, with a morning soaking of soil in dry weather.

Outdoors it takes about six to seven weeks from planting to first budding. Then you might give a booster shot of liquid plant food. From mid-May plantings you can get bloom from early July through all of frost-free October—a respectable span for any annual crop. I don't think it worthwhile to store tubers; they are inexpensive enough to let go with frost so I avoid the tiresome storing routine.

Where trees are surface-rooting, tuberous begonias in pots give the appearance of bedding. To bloom they must have protection from wind and shifting light, not deep shade. GEORGE TALOUMIS PHOTO

Caladiums with colorful foliage, the tubers started in pots, are set out to brighten a long stretch of dark-green pachysandra. GEORGE TALOUMIS PHOTO

My tuberous begonias have decorated the foreground of the apple-tree garden where the early morning sun catches them. They have been interspersed with myrtle under the hawthorn at the west, and on the south with Christmas ferns in the Round Garden, where the spring light is diffused by a *high-pruned* dogwood tree. Pots and bulb pans are variously placed at front and back doors and, on occasion, decorate the screened porch, but there is too little light there for bud formation over a long period.

The coolest-looking plant there is for a shaded place in summer is surely the caladium. In pots on the edge of a terrace or in a shadowed bed close by, *C.* 'Candidum' in green and white has the same pleasant effect on me as a witch-hazel-soaked cloth pressed to the forehead on a blazing day.

You can start the dormant tuberous roots of caladiums the same way you do the begonia corms or plant in 4-inch pots at the start. My own preference, as I have indicated, is the florist's ready-made method. Don't put caladiums outdoors until it is really warm for they are touchy about cold. Here it would hardly be safe until after May fifteenth. If you have a ferny place, caladiums will look charming there and appear even cooler than by themselves. Of course, you could have bright-color-leaved forms but so many other plants are colorful, I like to let caladiums play the green-and-white role of cooler.

BULBS FOR SPRING, FOR SUMMER

The spring-flowering bulbs flourish in late winter and early spring sunshine with shade after foliage ripens. The summer-flowering types do well in light shade or in an open place with good light but little sun. Plant all bulbs with tips at depth indicated.

Name	Height	Description	Culture	Remarks
Bulbs for Spring				
Chionodoxa luciliae Glory-of-the-snow	4–5"	Delicate blue or white flowers in short racemes.	Plant 3–4" deep; increases freely.	Nice, but not one of my indispensables; recommended for earliness, even before Dutch crocuses.
Crocus species		March	Plant 4–5" deep in sheltered locations with winter sun to get late-winter bloom; fine under shrubs.	The species are grand colonizers, pretty even in mixture; don't plant in lawn.
chrysanthus	3–6"	Golden, rounded blooms, many varieties.		

	Height			
sieberi		Lilac flowers, or lilac and white, very early.		
tomasinianus		Silvery buds open to amethyst flowers, orange stigmas.		
Daffodils, see *Narcissus*				
Dogtooth-violets, see *Erythronium*				
Dutch Hybrids.	6–8″	More gardenesque and a little later than species.	These have a nice formality for single or double row plantings along walks, or in a colony under east windows.	My favorites are the lavender 'Pickwick', white 'Peter Pan', and 'Yellow Mammoth'. They last for years.
Eranthis hyemalis Winter-aconite	5–6″	Yellow buttercup blooms, sometimes Jan., usually early Feb.–Mar. followed by lacy green umbrellas lasting until June, then disappearing.	Obtain tubers late Aug. or Sept.; soak overnight; plant 2″ deep; water well first autumn.	Earliest blooms open in a southern location, next a sun-warmed house wall, under shrubs. *Not to be missed;* carefree after first autumn.

Name	Height	Description	Culture	Remarks
Erythronium Dogtooth-violet or Trout-lily	6–12"	Brief enchanting turkscap bloom, yellow, white, pink, lavender, Mar.	Plant 3" deep in rich soil not likely to dry out.	Masses appeared on the brook bank and above, overrunning a bed of violets, definitely for naturalizing.
Galanthus elwesii Snowdrops	8"	Upright form with white flowers, good aconite companion, often blooms before snow melts.	Plant a lot (25 or so) of either kind in one patch for good effect; 4" deep.	Plant next a house wall for earliest bloom, but not in heavy ground-covers, all right among myrtle plants.
nivalis		Less formal look, for woodland plantings.		
Glory-of-the-snow, see *Chionodoxa*				
Grape-hyacinth, see *Muscari*				

Hyacinthus Hyacinth	15"	Marvelously fragrant blue, pink, white, or yellow for early Apr. Weather-resistant, absolutely indispensable.	Plant 8–10" deep in well-drained location; deep setting helps prevent flopping in rain; place 8" apart to allow room for annual plants.	I like repeated colonies of pale blue 'Myosotis', 'Delft Blue', or purple 'King of the Blues' between groupings of pale and deep yellow daffodils in the border. 'City of Haarlem' a handsome big yellow; 'Pink Pearl', lovely.
Iris reticulata Winter Iris	6"	Purple with yellow markings; fragrant, for Feb.–Mar.	Plant 3" deep in a dry, sheltered place.	Satisfying very early flower if it likes you but not one of the most dependable.
Lemon-squill, see *Puschkinia*				
Leucojum vernum Spring Snowflake	10–15"	Green-tipped white bells for late spring rather than summer, usually blooms with *Scilla hispanica*.	Plant 3" deep in colonies.	Attractive addition to the wealth of pretty, small bulbs, not essential like hyacinths!

Name	Height	Description	Culture	Remarks
Muscari Grape-hyacinth	6–9″	Mid-April or earlier; upside-down bunches of grapes, blue or white.	Plant 3″ deep, disappears after bloom; then produces winter-hardy grassy foliage.	'Heavenly Blue' good, reliable shade endurance.
Narcissus Daffodils	3–18″	Pale and deep yellows, whites; select early varieties, trumpets and flatcups mid-April; remember flowers face *toward* the sun.	Plant miniatures 2″ deep; trumpets and flatcups 9–10″ deep to slow up propagations which decreases bloom. Bulbs require sunlight to bloom and ripen foliage. Avoid planting under evergreens or in midst of ivy or pachysandra. Never remove foliage until it flops.	Bulbs last for years here under open deciduous trees where winter and early spring sun is strong. Right after bloom I fertilize with superphosphate or bonemeal and unleached wood ashes from fireplace; this supplies the essential potash.

Puschkinia scilloides Lemon-squill	1"	Tiny blue-lined white flowers, mignonette fragrance in March.	Plant 2–3" deep.	Pretty, hardly important.
Scilla sibirica Siberian squill	4–6"	Blue, late Mar.	Plant 3–4" deep; spreads freely.	Also good for naturalizing; 'Spring Beauty', intensely blue variety; one of the best.
hispanica (*campanulata*) Spanish squill Wood-hyacinth	20"	May, pink, lavender, white.	Plant 4" deep, multiplies generously.	Indispensable, looks rather like a thin hyacinth; pleasing in mixture.
Snowdrops, see *Galanthus*				
Squill, see *Scilla*				
Spring Snowflake, see *Leucojum*				
Trout-lily, see *Erythronium*				

Name	Height	Description	Culture	Remarks
Tulipa species Tulip		April	Plant all these botanicals 5″ deep in well-drained locations.	Bloom on most species comes before or with earliest daffodils in April; most bulbs do not "run out." Mixture of these 4–8″ species offers many surprises.
clusiana	8–10″	Outer petals cherry red, inside white, mid to late April; withstands spring rain and summer shade.		
fosteriana	12″	Crimson dark base; follows *kaufmanniana*.		Taller 'Red Emperor' and 'Yellow Empress', charming together.
greigii	10–12″	Orange-scarlet, dark basal blotch, a little later than *fosteriana*.		Greigii hybrids here in mixture in deep summer shade; last for years.

Tulipa continued *kaufmanniana*	4–6″	White to yellow, streaked carmine outside, large and open, among first to bloom.		Some lovely varieties as 'Fritz Kreisler', soft apricot.
praestans 'Fusilier'	10″	Light red, early April, lovely cluster-flowering type.		My bulbs of this ran out after second year; probably not planted deep enough, will try again.
"Earlies"	12–15″	Single and double types, all tulip colors; before trumpet daffodils.	Half-and-half shade; plant 8″ deep.	Good earliest singles: white 'Diana', scarlet 'De Wet', yellow 'Mon Tresor', rose 'Proserpine'. Early double: orange-salmon 'El Toreador', other doubles a little later.
Winter-aconite, see *Eranthis*				
Wood-hyacinth, see *Scilla*				

Name	Height	Description	Culture	Remarks
Bulbs for Summer				
Caladium	6–24″	Grow these for leaves, not flowers. Green-and-white or green, pink, and red foliage available.	Set well-started plants in a shaded garden bed. For a terrace, buy plants or start your own 4 to 6 weeks before your last frost date.	Candidum' is a lovely green-and-white, beautiful with ferns.
Lilium auratum Goldband Lily	5–6′	White with yellow band, spotted purple and crimson, Aug.	Plant 8″ deep; half-shade.	Fragrant Japanese lily.
canadense Meadow Lily	3–5′	Yellow to pale orange, brown spotted, bell-shaped down-facing flower.	Light to half-shade; plant 6″ deep; soil must not be dry.	Beautiful native for midsummer.

candidum Madonna Lily	3'	Pure white for late June, trumpet-shaped.	Plant as soon as you can get it; covered with only 1" of soil mixed with lime and wood ashes. Keep damp first autumn.	All lilies require good drainage. This old-fashioned favorite is choice for June.
hansonii	4–5'	Orange-yellow, brown spots, for June.	Plant 8" deep, half to light shade.	From Japan, fragrant.
martagon album Martagon Lily	3'	White turkscap form, mid-June.	Plant spring 3–4" deep.	This white is superior to purple-pink species; once established in woodland, it is forever.
Mid-Century Hybrids	3–5'	Late June onward, upward or outward facing lilies; various colors.	Plant 5–6" deep.	Excellent propagators; golden, 3-foot 'Joan Evans' fine here in quite deep shade; lemon-yellow 4-foot 'Prosperity' lovely.
philadelphicum Wood Lily	3'	Orange, spotted purple, June–July.	Plant 3" deep, full-light or half-shade.	Beautiful native lily for dry or moist soil; often grows at edge of woodland.

Name	Height	Description	Culture	Remarks
Lilium continued *speciosum album*	3–4'	August into Sept.	Plant 6" deep.	Indestructible here. 'White Champion' very handsome.
rubrum	3–4'			The "true" pink lily, fine with midday shade.
superbum American Turkscap Lily	3–7'	Nodding dark-orange-to-red flowers, spotted brown; July.	Plant 6" deep in moist acid soil; for open woodland.	Handsome native.
testaceum Nankeen Lily	7'	Apricot to yellow, pink-flushed, June–July.	Plant 5" deep, half-shade.	Not particular about soil.
tigrinum Tiger Lily	5'	Orange to salmon, spotted black.	Plant 3–4" deep, light to quite deep shade.	Volunteered here in front of big clethra bushes in wild garden; very handsome July–Aug.; needed staking as it reached toward light.

| Tuberous *Begonia* | 12–18″ | Ruffled double and rose forms, picotee and multiflora types for bedding or hanging baskets; white, pink, red, yellow, orange. | To start your own indoors, 8 weeks before last frost date, press into a flat of damp peat moss; move to 4″ pots when well rooted. Outdoors in garden or on terrace give light not dark shade with a little morning or afternoon sun. | Buy started plants if you can of both bedding and hanging-basket types. I plant directly in rich garden soil and spray with Karathane if any sign of mildew. Stake tall varieties; cut for flower arrangements. |

A pleasant shaded sitting area is developed in opened-up woodland with ferns and evergreens on each side of a wide path of irregular flagstones, with thyme in the crevices. PAUL E. GENEREUX PHOTO

FLOWERS AND FERNS
FOR WOODLAND SHADE

Exciting Snow-to-Frost Possibilities

Yellow violets, lavender primroses, white bloodroot and snow trilliums, rosy cyclamens—those are the very early treasures that brighten my woodland garden while a walk there is still a pretty cold experience, for patches of snow still linger late in March. Almost as cold-daring is the skunk-cabbage, thrusting up its ornamental helmets along the banks of the brook, and the fiddleheads of ferns, hardly more than knobs on the surface of the soil among these braver plants. Only the gardener who provides shade can enjoy such woodland beauties as these, for all must be sheltered from the sun and all require the woodsy soil that accumulates under trees.

Ferns alone can make an exciting shade garden. *Above, left.* The glorious royal and maidenhair ferns. PUTNEY NURSERY INC. PHOTO. *Above, right.* The charming spring sight of unfolding fiddleheads. *Below.* The tall cinnamon fern, *O. cinnamomea,* in a narrow viburnum-shaded bed with false spikenard in bloom and an epimedium edging. GEORGE TALOUMIS PHOTOS

The snow trillium is a handsome member of a handsome clan that you might want to collect. This blooms early for me in box-elder shade. GEORGE TALOUMIS PHOTO

Woodland into Garden

If you have a property with a patch of woodland, you can have a fine time developing a garden there just as I did. If you love the wildflowers, but have a limited area for gardening, you can still enjoy many of them by preparing the soil well in any shady section, perhaps along a narrow strip between your house and your neighbor's, perhaps in a corner, or along the boundary where trees give you privacy but can also provide the shade necessary for wildflowers and ferns.

When I acquired my wooded piece it was just an overgrown thicket of trees. It took several years to make it into a woodland garden where I could grow ferns as well as wildflowers. First, a number of trees had to be removed to open up the areas; then the remaining wild cherry, pin oak, dogwood, and box elder were pruned high and open. Eventually, I developed a wandering path the length of the garden entered from the lawn and made of grass for easy mowing. (I used flagstones first but these needed a lot of clipping around to make them neat so I removed them and sowed grass seed.)

On each side of the path I planted ferns—particularly the tall cinnamon, the royal, and the lower Christmas fern, various wild-flowers, and some so-called cultivated ones, too, like daylilies and astilbes. What plants belong in a wild garden, what ones in your borders is really up to you. Perhaps you will want only native plants, a nice way to select. I myself don't claim a really pure intention in my woodland. Some plants—ferns, trilliums, and trout-lilies—only appear at home in that setting, others have pleased me in both locations—garden and woodland. Groundcover plants are essential; you don't want any bare spaces. I have planted the foamflower for this purpose, also epimediums even though neither spreads very fast. *Iris cristata* is suitable and sweet woodruff moves at a fine clip, also the volunteering wild lily-of-the-valley (*Maian-themum canadense*), the small, sweet white violet, and taller Canada violet. But nothing is more satisfactory for coverage than the almost evergreen Christmas ferns. I planted early narcissus among them and never have to be patient about removing the maturing foliage since the ferns come along quickly enough to conceal it.

Possibilities among the wildflowers are endless; you can even have a good time collecting one group, as primroses, trilliums, violets, and certainly ferns. Or you could plan a late-winter-to-frost flower-ing sequence, which appeals most to me, early yellow trout-lilies to

Yellow polyantha primroses for May bloom richly in light shade in woodland settings or borders. GEORGE TALOUMIS PHOTO

final blue gentians. If you have space but few trees and delight in wildflowers above all others, you can make a charming setting for them by planting the smaller-growing trees, such as the Carolina silverbell, flowering dogwood, fringetree, sassafras, witch-hazel, birch, and pussy willow. Then, put practically your all into soil preparation. It's a big but essential bother. Wildflowers need a deep accumulation of leafmold and humus, and mostly they need an acid condition as well as plenty of moisture, for the natural woodland is always slightly damp.

Soil and Plants

Just as a guide, and not to be unduly dogmatic, and following the recommendation of that knowledgeable plantsman Andre Viette, I'd suggest you improve the soil in the area where you plan to grow woods plants somewhat like this:

Spread 3 inches peat moss over the area to be planted.
Spread 2 inches of humus or compost or leafmold or a
  combination of these.
Sprinkle 1 cup long-lasting general fertilizer per square yard.
Sprinkle 1 cup superphosphate per square yard.

Work all this in to a depth of 8 to 10 inches.

(Similar additions will benefit your perennial plantings. For them 2 inches of peat moss should be adequate. You might also add 1½ cups lime per square yard if plants are known to require a sweet soil, as clematis, but when using lime it's wise to get a soil test first. Your county agricultural agent will test your soil for you, or you can do it yourself with a Sudbury Test Kit offered by some seedsmen.)

Now, where to get your first plants? I say first, because once ideal conditions of shade and soil are established, you will probably be amazed at what nature alone will introduce. To me she offered trout-lilies, Jack-in-the-pulpit, Solomons-seal both true and false, the very tall summer meadowrue, various ferns, the brook bank of skunk-cabbage interspersed with false hellebore (*Veratrum viride*), and so many other plants that now I'm not always sure which of us set out which, the marsh-marigolds being among the questionables.

Today, a number of nurseries specialize in wildflowers—plants and seeds. General catalogues also list them. You will find names and addresses of some firms familiar to me under Sources at the end of this book. You can also rescue plants from sites being bulldozed

Top, left. A clump of bloodroot, *Sanguinaria canadensis,* always surprises me with March flowers opening under laurel bushes. GEORGE TALOUMIS PHOTO. *Top, right.* The pale yellow-to-white Dutchmansbreeches with ferny foliage are amusing plants that need sweet soil, unlike most wildflowers. *Below.* Bunchberry, *Cornus canadensis,* with miniature white dogwood flowers in May and bright red summer-to-fall fruits is a choice, but difficult, evergreen groundcover for a shaded woodland area. Both, PUTNEY NURSERY, INC. PHOTO

The 6-foot white meadowrue, *Thalictrum polygamum,* is a lovely summer sight rising amid Christmas ferns under a wild cherry tree.
GEORGE TALOUMIS PHOTO

or collect them from the woods, but be sure to get the owner's permission first, and then dig judiciously; don't take *all* of a colony. Also bear in mind that many wildflowers are on conservation lists. The president of your state garden club can give you a list for your state. The names of presidents and their addresses are listed at the back of each issue of *The National Gardener* magazine.

Three reliable spring-blooming perennials for light open shade in woodland or border. *Top, left.* The handsome pink bleedinghearts with ferny foliage; *Top, right,* yellow columbines for a shade-to-sun stretch. *Below.* A fine colony of pink-blue Virginia bluebells at the base of my great apple tree with pale blue forget-me-nots in the foreground. GEORGE TALOUMIS PHOTOS

Under tall white birches a wealth of wildflowers makes a charming garden—wild blue phlox and purple creeping phlox, white blood-root, yellow primroses, pink and white epimedium, and orange geum. GEORGE TALOUMIS PHOTO

In addition to the plants of low stature, you will enjoy, as I have, various shrubs that thrive under the same shady conditions, and make lovely backgrounds and accents in your woodland—azaleas, sweet pepperbush, and blueberries, for instance. These are discussed in Chapter 9.

On the following pages then are charts from which you can choose flowers and ferns for your own woodland garden. Actually, I am offering only a limited list, for wildflowers, and ferns too, are legion. You will notice that I was not successful in a few cases, and my failures are duly noted! Mostly these wildlings are easy plants, likely to spread and unlikely to get things. Given proper conditions of shade, soil, and moisture, they will give you much pleasure.

WILDFLOWERS FOR YOUR SHADED WOODLAND

All of these plants, mostly native, thrive in light shade, particularly under high-pruned deciduous trees. If deeper shade is tolerated, that is specifically indicated. Many of these are on state conservation lists; find out before you collect. For rhododendrons, azaleas, and other suitable shrubs, see Shrub Chart following Chapter 9.

Name	Height in Inches	Color and Season	Culture	Remarks
Actaea pachypoda White Baneberry, Dolls-eyes	18–24	Feathery white flowers, May; conspicuous white berries; native.	Light to deep shade in leafmold.	Also *A. rubra* with red berries.
Adonis vernalis Pheasants-eye	15	Yellow flowers, almost 3 inches across, Mar.–Apr.	Woods soil. Sow seeds in fall.	One of the most welcome earlies, nice with snowdrops.
Anemone canadensis	24	White, June, native.	Light to quite deep shade for all.	Anemones sometimes difficult to transplant from woods, best to buy plants. *A. canadensis* strong spreader among rocks.
quinquefolia Wood Anemone	12	White, Apr.–May, native.		

				Introduced from Europe.
sylvestris Snowdrop Anemone	15	White, May–June.		
Anemonella thalictroides Rue Anemone	8	White, Apr.–May, native.		
Aquilegia canadensis American Columbine	12–18	Scarlet-and-gold jaunty "jester's caps," May–June, native.	Delightful in my woods in front of a bank of sweet pepperbush.	Other columbines, blue *A. caerulea* and yellow *A. chrysantha*, also prosper in light-shaded woodland, but have more of a garden look.
Arbutus, see *Epigaea*				
Arisaema triphyllum Jack-in-the-pulpit	12–18	Hooded green **or** green-and-brown blooms, Apr.–May; red berries in summer, native.	Light to deep shade with moisture.	Appeared and spread prolifically here; one of my essentials.
Aruncus sylvester Goats-beard	50	Large, plumy white panicles, June–July, native.	Best in moist situation.	Fernlike effect, handsome background plant or along a stream.

Name	Height in Inches	Color and Season	Culture	Remarks
Asarum europaeum European Wild Ginger	4–6	Thick, shining, rounded evergreen leaves; greenish-purple May blooms.	Light to fairly deep shade; rich acid soil; excellent groundcover.	Our native wild ginger (*A. canadense*) not evergreen; no showy flowers on any gingers.
shuttleworthii	6–8	June–July flowers; leaves mottled white, native.	Not reliably hardy north of Philadelphia.	Slow-growing.
Bishops-hat, see *Epimedium*				
Bleedingheart, see *Dicentra*				
Bloodroot, see *Sanguinaria*				
Bluebeads, see *Clintonia*				
Bluebell, see *Campanula*				
Bluets, see *Houstonia*				
Bunchberry, see *Cornus*				

Caltha palustris Marsh-marigold	12–15	Yellow buttercups in Apr. followed by big spreading leaves, native.	Moist ground or shallow water; light to deep shade.	Fine early color in swamp area below cliff path; disappears in summer; some plants floated downstream in flood.
Campanula rotundifolia Bluebell, Harebell	15–18	Nodding bright blue flowers, wiry stems, June–frost.	Easy from seed; semishade; plant among rocks for a blue cascade.	Spreads readily; the bluebells of Scotland, naturalized in this country.
Canada Mayflower, see *Maianthemum*				
Cardinal-flower, see *Lobelia*				
Chimaphila maculata Spotted Pipsissewa	4–10	Nodding white to pinkish flowers, June–July; evergreen, native.	Rich acid soil, difficult to grow, possibly dependent on bacterial organisms in certain soils.	Charming, low white-veined green groundcover.

Name	Height in Inches	Color and Season	Culture	Remarks
Chimaphila continued umbellata Common Pipsissewa	5–12	Deep pink, waxen flowers, late June, evergreen.	Pine needle soil excellent.	Plain green leaves; both slow to spread.
Cimicifuga racemosa Snakeroot (See Color Section)	48–60	White wands; July–Aug. very showy, native.	Rather moist soil; light to quite deep shade.	Lovely here in front of hemlocks and gray stone wall, also with old-fashioned orange daylilies.
Claytonia virginica Spring Beauty	4–6	Delicate white-to-pink Mar.–June flowers, native.	Half-shade, acid leafmold.	Mark the plantings; this disappears in summer.
Clintonia borealis Bluebeads	7–15	Tiny yellow lilylike flowers, late May; blue fruit in Sept., native.	Half-shade, acid soil.	Broad, shiny green leaves and blue berries, an interesting plant.

Columbine, see *Aquilegia*

Cornus canadensis Bunchberry	5–8	Miniature white dogwood flowers early in May on creeping evergreen plants; bright red berries, native.	Rich, acid fairly moist soil. Prefers cool climate.	Not the easiest to establish but a charming plant worth struggling for.
Creeping Buttercup, see *Ranunculus*				
Cyclamen europaeum	3–4	Fragrant, deep rose-colored flowers, Aug.–Sept.; leaves mottled white.	Half-shade; plant corms in July with 1 inch of soil above them; mark the spots; plants not always in evidence.	If you like the florist's cyclamens, you will enjoy these smaller hardy treasures. Nice among rocks.
neapolitanum		Pink or white flowers, Sept.–frost, often before round marbled leaves appear.	2 inches of soil above corms.	

Name	Height in Inches	Color and Season	Culture	Remarks
Cyclamen continued *orbiculatum coum* Coum Cyclamen		Rose, red, or white, lovely late-winter or very early-spring surprise, Jan.–Apr.	1 inch of soil above corms.	
Cypripedium acaule Pink Lady-slipper	6–15	Showy pink moccasins in June on single stems rising from two basal leaves, native.	Requires a strongly acid soil, containing a special fungus, difficult.	Beautiful colony above the brook under the cliff but total disappearance after 2 years, the usual experience I am told.
calceolus pubescens Yellow Lady-slipper	12–20	One or more bright yellow, fragrant flowers, May–June, on stems above large oval leaves, native.	Light to rich moist neutral or alkaline soil, not acid.	Easiest of the lady-slippers, really amenable.
reginae Showy Lady-slipper	24	Rose-flushed white flowers, late May–July, native.	Moist soil.	Not too easy.

Dicentra cucullaria Dutchmans-breeches	6–10	Pale yellow to white "pantaloons" late Apr.–May, disappears in summer, native.	Humusy soil, nice for a slope, needs lime.	A lovely stand of this under my cliff finally disappeared altogether; too dry and unfertile perhaps, and too acid.
eximia Fringed Bleedingheart	12–15	Nodding heart-shaped rose flowers, spring to fall, native.	Needs moisture.	Graceful, ferny foliage, lovely thing, also likes sunshine; excellent groundcover in woodland. (Taller bleedingheart, *D. spectabilis*, better for borders.)
Dodecatheon meadia Shooting Star	10	Showy pink flowers, suggest the cyclamen, May–June, native.	Acid soil, well drained.	Attractive groundcover that could stretch from shade to sun.
Dogtooth-violet, see *Erythronium*				
Dolls-eyes see *Actaea*				

Name	Height in Inches	Color and Season	Culture	Remarks
Dutchmans-breeches, see *Dicentra*				
Epigaea repens Trailing-arbutus	3	White-tinted, richly scented flowers; Apr.–May, native.	Plant in strongly acid soil dug from under pines or hemlocks; mulch with pine needles, moisture important.	Such a treasure but I couldn't please it, not an easy wildling.
Epimedium grandiflorum Bishops-hat See also Groundcover Chart	8–12	Lovely delicate white, pink, lavender varieties May–June, light green heart-shaped leaves, evergreen.	Half-shade, moist soil, will stand some sun, good for both woodland and border.	Mine grows in quite heavy shade near the brook, *not to be missed*, but they are slow to spread.
Erythronium americanum Trout-lily, Dogtooth-violet	6–10	Little yellow lilylike flowers, Mar. or early Apr., leaves mottled, native.	Rich moist leafmold; grand spreader.	Every time the brook overflows, a new stretch appears.

Eupatorium coelestinum Hardy Ageratum	2	Good lavender or white, Aug.–Oct.; nice fall color, native.	Needs moisture.	Weedy grower, plant where you want quick coverage, good cut flower. Useful color with chrysanthemums.
False Solomons-seal, see *Smilacina*				
Foamflower, see *Tiarella*				
Forget-me-not, see *Myosotis*				
Galax aphylla		White spike flowers, May–June; evergreen heart-shaped leaves, native.	Light to deep shade, acid soil, moisture.	Clumps flourish here with ferns; good groundcover particularly with azaleas and rhododendrons.
Gaultheria procumbens, see Groundcover Chart Wintergreen				

Name	Height in Inches	Color and Season	Culture	Remarks
Gentiana andrewsii Closed Gentian	12–16	Rich blue-purple "bottles," Sept.; never fully opens, native.	Half-shade, prefers marsh or bog location.	Not the easiest, but a fine end-of-season plant when it succeeds. Sow seed as soon as ripe.
Geranium maculatum Wild Geranium	15–18	Pink-lavender panicles late May–June, cut down after bloom, marvelous spreader, native.	Open light or light shade of bushes.	Edges my fern path with *Scilla hispanica*, lovely for almost a month. This is not the familiar true geranium, *Pelargonium*.
Ginger, see *Asarum*				
Goats-beard, see *Aruncus*				
Hardy Ageratum, see *Eupatorium*				
Harebell, see *Campanula*				
Hepatica americana Round-lobed Hepatica	6	Lilac-white flowers Mar.–Apr. among the first; evergreen foliage, native.	Dry acid soil, quite deep shade here.	Self-sows freely; makes pretty colonies in shady corners or interplanted with ferns.

Hesperis matronalis Sweet Rocket	36–40	Loose night-fragrant racemes, white or lavender; June–Sept.	Any soil, any location, light to deep shade here.	Self-sowing biennial; start with a white and violet seed mixture.
Houstonia caerulea Bluets, Quaker Ladies	3	Tiny blue to white flowers, Apr.–May, native.	Moist soil, open woodlands.	Rapid grower, along stream; also a rather darling bother in my lawn.
Iris cristata, I. *gracilipes,* see Perennial Chart				
Jack-in-the-pulpit, see *Arisaema*				
Lady-slipper, see *Cypripedium*				
Lilium, see Bulb Chart				
Lobelia cardinalis Cardinal-flower	24–36	Scarlet spikes, July–Sept, short-lived perennial, native.	Moist, rich soil; light to deep shade edge of bog or pool.	Fine deep-summmer color; protect with mulch in winter; sometimes disappears then.

Name	Height in Inches	Color and Season	Culture	Remarks
Lobelia continued *siphilitica* Blue Lobelia	12–36	Showy, bright-blue spikes, Aug.–Sept., native.	Not so particular about soil; shade or sun, moisture.	Effective late-summer blue, rampant, also a white form.
Maianthemum canadense Canada Mayflower, Wild Lily-of-the-valley	4	White for May, not showy, but charming, native.	Acid soil, moist or dry, good under evergreen shrubs.	Volunteered under heavy beech and oak shade on top of my cliff.
Marsh-marigold, see *Caltha*				
May-apple, see *Podophyllum*				
Meadowrue, see *Thalictrum*				
Mertensia virginica Virginia Bluebells	15	Pink-blue flowers for 2 to 3 Apr.-to-May weeks; then plant disappears, native.	Light to deep shade; acid soil, self-sows readily.	Associate with bleeding-hearts, ferns, and early daffodils in woodland or border; among the loveliest; ferns fill in vacancies after disappearance.

Mitchella repens Partridge-berry	trailing	Tiny fragrant pink-to-white June blooms; red berries late summer; glossy evergreen leaves, native.	Light to deep shade; woods soil, slightly acid.	Gather berries as soon as ripe for terrariums; birds love them; rapid grower once started.
Myosotis scorpioides, see Groundcover Chart Forget-me-not				
Oconee-bells, see *Shortia*				
Partridge-berry, see *Mitchella*				
Pheasants-eye, see *Adonis*				
Phlox divaricata, see Groundcover Chart				
Pipsissewa, see *Chimaphila*				
Podophyllum peltatum May-apple	12–18	Fragrant white Apr.–May flowers, almost hidden by big leaves; yellow fruit, late summer, native.	Rich soil, light to deep shade.	Roots, leaves, seeds said to be poisonous, but not fruit! Good carpeting plant.

Name	Height in Inches	Color and Season	Culture	Remarks
Polygonatum biflorum Small Solomons-seal	24–36	Greenish May–June bell flowers strung along arching stems, native.	Light to deep shade, rich woods soil.	*P. commutatum*, Great Solomons-seal, to 6 ft., too large and coarse for most situations.
Primrose, see *Primula*				
Primula Primrose			Leafmold and moisture for all, light not deep shade; strong hose spray in hot weather to prevent red spider.	One of the shade gardener's grand opportunities; you could even collect primroses, lovely along a stream or massed under a tree; also excellent garden plants.
auricula Alpine Primrose	6–8	Hybrids in various colors, yellow or white eye, in umbels; Apr.–May.	Top-dressing of limestone advised, give winter protection to avoid roots heaving.	Strong flower stems rise from evergreen leaf rosette, handsome strain of Giant Hybrids. For shaded rock garden or north slope.

denticulata Himalayan Primrose	12	Lavender, pink, or purple flowers in dense globes on stout stems right after snow melts before foliage develops.	Best where winters are cold.	Reliable and enchanting. A white form has slightly larger flowers in looser heads.
japonica Japanese Primrose (Candelabra Group)	12–18	White, red, pink flowers in whorls spaced out on tall stalks. Brilliant display May–July.	A really damp situation, streamside or low place in woods.	One of the tall Asiatic primulas; related species 2 to even 3½ feet, bloom from early summer to Aug. according to species, pastel shades of apricot, clear yellow, magenta-purple, etc.
x *juliana*	4–6	Very hardy named hybrids, enduring heat and dryness better than most species. Deep red, lilac, rich purple, white. May.	Moderately moist humusy soil in part-shade or deeper.	Stoloniferous, hence mat-forming. Mixed varieties usually harmonious.

Name	Height in Inches	Color and Season	Culture	Remarks
Primula continued *polyantha* Bunch Primrose	9–12	For May; available in separate colors—blue, crimson, gold, pink, also Pacific Giants mixed strain. Leaves handsome and lasting, good edging plant.	Rich soil, light covering of leaves in winter. Divide every second year after blooming.	Delightful old horticultural group, in English gardens for centuries, unknown in wild; some dwarfs popular, easily raised from seed.
veris Cowslip	8	Fragrant yellow flowers with orange eye in May; "hose-in-hose" type has double corolla.	This and *P. vulgaris* may be more tender than others.	Charming under my apple tree with Virginia bluebells.
vulgaris (acaulis) English Primrose	6–9	Yellow to purple early Apr.–May flowers, lightly fragrant, each on one stem but in quantity.	Tend to work way out of soil, divide and replant as needed; water deeply in dry spells.	Blue Beauties, rich blue-to-violet strain.
Quaker Ladies, see *Houstonia*				

Ranunculus repens Creeping Buttercup	4–8	Bright-yellow flowers May–Aug.; a showy volunteer that needs control.	Damp to wet soil.	Weedy, vinelike growth, good coverage here in wild garden and bog.
Sanguinaria canadensis Bloodroot	6–8	Single white flowers Mar.–May; broad, feltlike leaves, native.	Light to deep shade, rich soil.	Here under laurel, disappears in summer; valued for its very early, evanescent flowers.
Shortia galacifolia Oconee-bells	8	White, early-May nodding flowers, ever-green foliage, native.	Light to deep shade; moist acid soil.	Choice plant for naturalizing; here under dogwood.
Skunk-cabbage, see *Symplocarpus*				
Smilacina racemosa False Solomons-seal	24–36	Terminal green-white pointed clusters; white-to-red fall berries, native.	Moist acid soil, naturalizes easily, may appear in your woods.	Striking woodland plant; this volunteered freely here, was most welcome. (See also *Polygonatum*.)

Name	Height in Inches	Color and Season	Culture	Remarks
Snakeroot, see *Cimicifuga*				
Sweet Rocket, see *Hesperis*				
Symplocarpus foetidus Skunk-cabbage	12–24	Inconspicuous hooded flowers, March; handsome big leaf clumps; no smell unless cut, native.	Moist or wet soils.	Green plants slowly open very early on stream bank, great favorite; cut back as it fades and disappears in summer.
Thalictrum aquilegifolium Meadowrue	36	Columbine-like foliage, fluffy white or purplish flowers, May–June.	Rich humusy soil, moisture.	All meadowrues are charming open plants for border or woodland, ferny foliage; fine to cut.
polygamum Tall Meadowrue	60–70	Dainty white flowers, in airy panicles, July–Sept.		Unexpected guest under the wild cherry tree, needs staking, handsome.
speciosum (glaucum) Dusty Meadowrue	36–48	Fuzzy yellow slightly fragrant flowers, blue-gray foliage, lovely in summer bouquets.		

Tradescantia virginiana Foamflower	6–12	White flowers, Apr.–July.	Partial to quite deep shade here; moisture.	Spreads rather slowly in my woods; choice plant, good groundcover.
Tiarella cordifolia Spiderwort	15–24	Purple, white, June–Aug.; rests after bloom, cut down then, fall crop follows, rushlike leaves, native.	Light to quite deep shade, flowers closed by afternoon, more open next morning.	Modern varieties also lovely—white, violet-tinted, pink. Here beside the brook, and under a cherry tree, white 'Iris Pritchard', 'Purple Dome', pink 'Pauline'. Don't miss these!
Trillium cernuum Nodding Trillium	9–15	White or pink May flowers.	Light to quite deep shade here; rich moist soil; naturalize nicely under trees.	Among loveliest of native wildflowers; you might like to collect these; several others available.
erectum Wake Robin	9–18	Red-purple May flowers.		

Name	Height in Inches	Color and Season	Culture	Remarks
Trillium continued				
grandiflorum Snow Trillium	10–20	Large white Apr.–May flowers, turning pink; very handsome.		
luteum Yellow Trillium	12	Pale-yellow May flowers; dark mottled leaves.		
undulatum Painted Trillium	8–15	White flowers brushed purple at base, showy red berries.		
Trout-lily, see *Erythronium*				
Viola blanda Sweet White Violet	2–5	Tiny, fragrant white Apr.–May flowers.	Light shade, good for low wet places.	All these natives are good woodland ground-covers; violets are fun to collect, many others can be found.

canadensis Canada Violet	12	Fragrant, blue-tinged white flowers, recurrent May–July bloom, sometimes in fall.	Deep shade.	Good choice for long bloom; blooms earliest for me next house wall.
cucullata Common Blue Violet	6–10	Good foliage, lavender flowers, some bloom all summer.	Light shade, longer stems in a moist location.	Thrives even in a wet place. Excellent garden plant.
palmata Wood Violet	8–12	Deeply lobed leaves, purple flowers, Apr.–June.	Deep shade.	Will stand a fairly dry spot.
pedata Birdfoot Violet	4–6	Apr.–May two-toned purple flowers; may repeat in fall.	Light shade or sun, acid sandy soil.	Leaves resemble a bird's footprint, upper petals violet, lower ones lavender.
pubescens Downy Yellow Violet	8–12	Bright yellow, Apr.–May flowers, long stems.	Light rather dry soil, light to deep shade.	Several small flowers, not showy.

Name	Height in Inches	Color and Season	Culture	Remarks
Viola continued *rotundifolia* Roundleaf Violet	4–6	Fine early yellow purple-striped flowers, nice surprise following the snow, native.	For moist cool woods, half to deep shade.	Thrives under shrubs and evergreens
Virginia Bluebells, see *Mertensia*				
White Baneberry, see *Actaea*				
Wild lily-of-the-valley, see *Maianthemum*				
Wintergreen, see *Gaultheria*				

FERNS FOR WOODLAND AND BORDER

Shade offers a fine opportunity for ferns; in fact, you can have a lovely shade garden with ferns alone. Here are a few of the many I have grown with great pleasure—the deciduous (D), evergreen (E), and semievergreen (Semi) types. Ferns combine beautifully with flowers, and they are also useful in concealing the departure of plants that die down after **blooming, as bulbs, some perennials in borders, and also various wildflowers. All listed here are native.**

Name	Height in Inches	Type	Culture	Behavior and Appearance	Remarks
Adiantum pedatum Maidenhair Fern	12–20	D	For light to quite dense shade; moist, *neutral* rich leafmold, drainage important.	Creeping, unique, dainty circular lacy tops; wiry dark stems. Most beautiful of all.	Early appearance, light to medium green, lovely with spring wildflowers or facing down shrubs.
Athyrium filix-femina Lady Fern	12–36	D	Dry to wet woods; partial shade or full sun.	Yellow-green to medium green, older leaves brownish, finely cut, creeping.	Adaptable, almost too strong in volunteering; here a carpet under white birch, not for a small garden.
Bladder or Bulblet Fern, see *Cystopteris*					

Name	Height in Inches	Type	Culture	Behavior and Appearance	Remarks
Christmas Fern, see *Polystichum*					
Cinnamon Fern, see *Osmunda*					
Cystopteris bulbifera Bladder Fern, Bulblet	18–30	D	Neutral or sweet, not acid soil; best on weathered limestone.	Long narrow tapering fronds; pinkish stems; yellow-green fronds produces baby ferns from bulblets; amusing to children.	For rock garden or to shade soil for clematis or other lime-lovers; naturalizes readily, appears 4 to 6 weeks after fragile bladder fern.
fragilis Fragile Bladder Fern	4–12	D	Sensitive to drought; may discolor; good on rocks and ledges, neutral to slightly acid soil.	Deeply toothed, green; spreads into crevices.	Early croziers uncurl before other ferns, late Mar.; good cover for earliest bulbs.

Name	Size	Type	Culture	Description	Remarks
Dryopteris intermedia Shield Fern Evergreen Wood Fern	15–30	E	Moist, acid, rich humus..	Deeply cut, dark-green prickly fronds.	Shield ferns indispensable. This one late to emerge, so excellent with bulbs.
marginalis Shield Fern Leather Wood Fern	12–20	E		Blue-green, evergreen fronds in vase form; very lovely.	Firm texture, not toothed, fruit dots underneath along the margins of leaflet.
noveboracensis New York Fern	8–24	E	Adaptable, late in coming up, about mid-May, turns brown early.	Shallow creeper, delicate light green, somewhat invasive.	Excellent groundcover; fronds taper both ends; lovely contrast to deeper greens.
spinulosa Shield Fern Toothed Wood Fern	14–28	E D	Sterile fronds. Fertile fronds.	Circular clumps, lighter green than *D. intermedia*, very lovely crown.	Volunteered under my apple tree and along wall, also edge of bog garden; lacy but less so than *D. intermedia*.
Interrupted Fern, see *Osmunda*					
Lady Fern, see *Athyrium*					

Name	Height in Inches	Type	Culture	Behavior and Appearance	Remarks
Maidenhair Fern, see *Adiantum*					
Matteuccia pensylvanica Ostrich Fern	36–60	D	Shade to full sun if near water; deep rich soil, moist to wet; for streamsides.	Plumy vase form but creeps by ropelike stolons even under paving; turns brown early.	Not for refined locations, hard to eliminate but attractive where plenty of room; does look like an ostrich plume.
New York Fern, see *Dryopteris*					
Osmunda cinnamomea Cinnamon Fern	24–48	D	Requires rich acid soil and moisture, native to bogs.	Mighty grower where conditions suit; crown; looks tropical.	Fine bold accent; showiest fiddleheads; "cinnamon stick" sterile fronds; lovely with daylilies; allow 3 to 4 ft. spread for all osmundas.
claytoniana Interrupted Fern	30–36	D	Deep rich soil, acid, moist, native in swampy places, will endure sun.	Somewhat coarse fronds, good specimen plant, crown, yellow-green to dark.	Fertile fronds "interrupted" by separate branchlets of spore cases; interesting growth.

regalis Royal Fern	24–48	D	Light to dense shade; moist acid soil; in drier locations only with special care.	Young fronds wine-red; brown spore clusters like flowers, vase form fine for contrast; native in swampy places.	Graceful for a bank or as an accent; mixes well with cinnamon and interrupted, or with Japanese iris and astilbe, deserves name, really massive.
Ostrich Fern, see *Matteuccia*					
Polystichum acrostichoides Christmas Fern	15–30	Semi	Fairly damp, rich leafmold, but adaptable; here under dogwoods and witch-hazel beneath cliff.	Refined, crown spreads slowly fine groundcover, evergreen until midwinter.	Edge of my woodland interplanted with narcissus; elsewhere with white violets for groundcover and with tulips. Indispensable.
Royal Fern, see *Osmunda*					
Shield Fern, see *Dryopteris*					
Wood Ferns, see *Dryopteris*					

Astilbes, this one 'Deutschland', are among the most rewarding of all shade plants, flowering well from June to August in open light or, for me, in the quite deep shade of a neighbor's tree, the fine foliage also an asset. GEORGE TALOUMIS PHOTO

7

CHOICE PERENNIALS
THAT BLOOM IN SHADE

*The Obliging Three
and Many Others*

One way to discover the perennials that will flourish and bloom
in shade is to have shade gradually develop above them. If this
had not happened here, I probably would not have discovered
the shade tolerance of such fine plants as the balloon-flower,
baptisia, Chinese delphinium, at least one aster, globeflower,
coralbells, various irises, and certainly not peonies, which I supposed
required uninhibited sunshine. Although sunshine poured down
on the original plantings, in due course, it was considerably miti-
gated by the growth of various flowering trees, and also by the development of shrubs that were small when the perennials made their
first appearance.

In any case, shade gardening is not a matter of rule but of
experiment. There are so many variables, and shade is only one
factor of culture, others being soil, drainage, tree roots, winter
temperatures, exposure to wind, degrees of dryness and moisture.

The indispensable
Christmas-rose, *Helleborus
niger,* with white flowers
pink-tinted as they age, and
evergreen leaves, blooms in
light to quite deep shade,
some years opening in a
warm January but usually
not till February, and
staying beautiful for weeks
—the earliest perennial in
shade. PAUL E. GENEREUX
PHOTO

Too often when plants don't develop properly in a shady site, it's
not lack of light but dryness and infertility that are the deterrents.
So consider all this as you select perennials for your shaded site
and try to provide the generally good conditions that let shade
be an asset and not a detriment.

First to open here are the Christmas-roses; you really must
have a few plants of these almost-evergreen perennials and within
window view. Depending on weather, the buds you can see nest-
ling down in the crown of the plants will push up and open late in
January or early in February, not, alas, for Christmas. These hellebores are the finest of winter flowers and once the white cups open,
despite snow, they stay fresh and crisp, gradually turning a delicate
rosy hue. Not until April do I cut them off. I have particularly

enjoyed them in association with Christmas ferns and the bright little yellow aconites, all under the leafless silverbell-tree and burgeoning Cornelian-cherry. Here summer shade for the Christmas-roses is almost "deep."

SPRING BLOOM

April–May. The spring months are now full of color. Under all the deep-rooted late-leafing trees, along with the bulbs that revel in early sunshine and summer shade, come some lovely April- and May-blooming perennials. In association with the early narcissus they are particularly delightful. One favorite grouping of mine— I have repeated it in every garden I have ever had—consists of tall pink bleedinghearts, Virginia bluebells, yellow globeflower and leopardsbane, hybrid columbines—white, yellow, and lavender— and yellow cowslips. All these are carpeted with self-sowing, blue, biennial forget-me-nots with patches of white rockcress at one end of the bed. The whole is edged with transitional coralbells that carry color into June and summer. At the back, interrupted and cinnamon ferns, not so eager to appear as the early perennials, gradually unfurl their fronds to hide the disappearing bluebells and the June shabbiness of the bleedinghearts.

To this favorite association of mine, you may want to add the small, enchanting, golden-anthered, purple pasqueflower. Or perhaps you can tuck it in beside a little flight of rock steps where it will look charming. If you have a fairly large shaded area, moist to wet, where a handsome bold-foliaged accent will be suitable, plant the May-flowering bergenia. It will tolerate quite deep shade, indeed does not like the sun at all.

Then there is brunnera, formerly considered an anchusa, with delicate blue sprays of spring bloom rising above foliage that will be coarse and heavy as spring passes into summer. At one time I had a grand bed of this on a bank under a cherry tree but there the persistent woodchucks won out and I had to substitute.

For a May–June edging plant, the white hardy candytuft is un-surpassed. Where there is space, I favor the 12-inch evergreen species, *Iberis sempervirens,* that spreads to 15 inches. I have it surrounding a long shrub border where one side is fairly sunny, the other fairly shady. For limited quarters the cultivars 'Autumn Snow', which re-peats in fall, 'Little Gem', and 'Purity', all about 6 inches high, are good choices.

Various irises thrive in shade. The early little lavender or white crested iris makes a nice groundcover, and the tall yellow flag, *Iris pseudacorus,* looks happy beside the brook, these two for May into June. If you are fond of iris, you can grow a number of others in shade, as the June-into-July Japanese with its handsome flat blooms for a moist not boggy place, the purple or white June Siberian with grassy foliage that I like to use for bold accent, and the small-flowered, wild blue flag, *I. versicolor,* that naturalized along the wet brook bank and blooms late in June. Of course German iris and some lesser-known species are absolutely sun-demanding and not suited to your shaded place.

A surprise to me was the good behavior of certain peonies in shade. The fragrant tree peonies, *Paeonia suffruticosa (Moutan),* definitely thrive in half-shade. These bloom mid-May on, about two weeks before the more familiar garden types, and hold their woody framework, for they are really shrubs. Mine grow protected from wind, and with just a little late-afternoon sun, at the edge of shade under the hawthorn tree. You can have white, pink, red, or white, or the yellow Lutea hybrids. I particularly like such yellows as 'Mme. Louise Henry', 'Alice Harding', 'L'Esper-ance', and 'Souvenir de Maxime Cornu'.

Louis Smirnow, a peony specialist, also recommends these for "half-shade to almost full-shade": pinks, 'Gosho Zakur' (Cherries of the Imperial Palace), and 'Tama Fuyow' (Jeweled Lotus); reds, 'Red Beauty' and 'Higurashi' (Twilight); purple, 'Hana Daijin' (Minister of Flowers), and 'Rimpow' (Sacred Bird). He thinks 'Stolen Heaven' the best white, but I found my 'Renkaku' (Flight of Cranes) a glistening marvel. If the names affright you,

don't be afraid to buy by color alone. (The Smirnow peony catalogue is in color; see Sources.) The Japanese tree peonies are also
listed as Chinese. Tree peonies are expensive but with you forever.
You sometimes come upon them in the overgrown tangles of old
gardens.

When Reginald Farrer, the plant explorer, saw Moutan peonies
for the first time (in 1914) on the mountainsides of Kansu
Province, China, he called them "the most overpoweringly superb
of hardy shrubs." I always recall his enthusiasm when my plants
open their tremendous yellow or white blooms in May with the long
flat planes of the white May-tree in bloom above them. Once well
planted, preferably in early fall, tree peonies are undemanding
except for deep watering in summer and permanent quarters;
moving about sets them back.

JUNE-TO-AUGUST ACCENTS

June, the end of spring, the start of summer, is a grand burgeoning
month, a time of transition. It could be the end of flowering time
at your place if you wish, with pleasure to be taken in green leafy
shade through the hot weather. But there are such grand summer
flowers, I always get trapped, especially among the many good
blues.

But first, let's consider the transition plants like the airy
white or rose coralbells that border the Apple-Tree Garden and
bloom luxuriously until August in a sun-to-shade ribbon. Even
without bloom, I enjoy those pretty crowns of foliage. Then there
is the plumy pink bleedingheart, *Dicentra eximia,* that does not
grow so tall as the old-fashioned May-flowering one, *D. spectabilis,*
but keeps going much longer, even to October.

In the same bed is the "permanent" gasplant, *Dictamnus,* handsome in June bloom and with fine enduring foliage of a lemony
fragrance in hot weather. (Strike a match to this some night, just

In light shade in front of a
wovenwood fence the white
gasplant, *Dictamnus albus,*
blooms in June; its excellent
foliage endures till frost.
GEORGE TALOUMIS PHOTO

under the bloom, and watch a child's amazement; the flash of light
won't hurt your plant.) My gasplant is white but there are also
a rose-pink and a purplish one.

Among yellows for shade is the evening-primrose, *Oenothera
fruticosa,* that readily takes up residence and spreads and spreads,
a few transplants eventually covering our neighborhood. The too-
little-known Carolina-lupine, *Thermopsis caroliniana,* has given me
much pleasure as an accent plant in a long border, and the
perennial foxglove, also overlooked, produces stalwart spikes of
pale-yellow bloom from June into July in quite deep shade here.

Summer blues are legion as my garden diaries indicate. The tall
Anchusa azurea needs half to light shade, a good back-of-the-
border plant for June to August. The Chinese delphinium, not
so spectacular as the giant hybrids, really biennial, is a pretty airy
thing, with intermittent bursts of color late June into July if you
plant it under sky shine. *Baptisia* with blue pea-shaped flowers in
June and fine foliage—such an asset—makes a good mid-border

The purple balloon-flower blooms here in quite deep shade under the silverbell-tree but it likes sunshine, too, and so is a good unifier for a shade-to-sun border. PAUL E. GENEREUX PHOTO

accent. More purple than blue is the fine-to-cut *Aster* x *frikartii* for June to frost, the various bluebells for June to October, and the balloon-flower, *Platycodon,* that continually sets buds deep in silverbell shade.

And what about phlox? I have heard reports that it is shade tolerant, especially if plants are not crowded but have good air circulation. The early white 'Miss Lingard' is recommended. Unfortunately, my own experience has not been good. Even in very light shade, plants grew spindly and mildewed unpleasantly, so I no longer attempt phlox. Perhaps your trial plantings will be more satisfactory.

The Hyacinth Hybrid foxgloves, *Digitalis,* with white-to-rose florets all round the stems, are effective biennials for a long stretch in border or woodland. GEORGE TALOUMIS PHOTO

THREE FOR SUMMERTIME

The lightly shaded garden need not be without color in **July and August.** For this season the daylilies are undoubtedly the showiest of all. These with hostas and astilbes have performed notably for me, the daylilies preferring sun but still tolerant of shade, while the astilbes and hostas plainly require shade.

Astilbes

The astilbes—perhaps you have called them spiraeas or meadow-sweet, not goatsbeard, I hope—produce from June to August

Early daffodils bloom at the edge of woodland in late-winter, early-spring sunshine before trees are in leaf; the summer shade is to their liking. NELSON GROFFMAN PHOTO

Left. Pink, yellow, and white azaleas bloom under high-pruned box-elder and birch with just a few hours of late afternoon sunlight. CHARLES MARDEN FITCH PHOTO. *Above, right*. A hanging basket of annual browallia, 'Silver Bells' and 'Blue Bells'. GEO. J. BALL, INC. PHOTO. *Center*. Pink *Begonia semperflorens,* one of the best annuals for shade. GEORGE TALOUMIS PHOTO. *Below Right*. *Hosta subcordata grandiflora,* an excellent perennial for shade. WAYSIDE GARDENS CO. PHOTO

Above left. Carefree Coleus are as colorful as flowers in shade above a rock wall. WALTER HARING PHOTO. *Right.* White snakeroot, a perennial that prefers the shade. *Below left.* The lovely new silverbell-tree, *Halesia vestita verticillata,* for April–May. Both, WAYSIDE GARDENS CO. PHOTOS. *Right, Phlox divaricata,* well fertilized and watered, blooms here in rich soil pockets under high-pruned, surface-rooting maples. WALTER HARING PHOTO

In the heat of summer an all-green garden with shifting sunshine is a serene sight. Here a great stretch of pachysandra grows to the left of the path, rhododendrons at the right, and the lawn flourishes beyond. NELSON GROFFMAN PHOTO

feathery fragrant spires, red, pink, or white, above ferny foliage that knows neither pest nor disease (but will brown quickly in drought). Beautiful from spring emergence to frost crispness, the plants are pleasing even out of bloom. I am fond of the whites, the 18-inch 'Avalanche' and somewhat taller 'Deutschland', the light-pink 'Peach Blossom' and deeper 'Rosy Veil', both to 2 feet. You may prefer 'Fanal' a fine 18-inch carmine, or 'Red Sentinel', a good background astilbe to 30 inches.

Astilbes prefer a rich moist soil and have reveled in beds near the brook along with ferns and Japanese iris, but to my amazement they also prospered handsomely in a dim corner under pine trees where one spring I planted some extras.

Daylilies

In that same untoward location, behold daylilies as floriferous as if the sun beat down upon them. That *was* a discovery, the result of my never discarding excess plants but sticking them *somewhere* when I really have too many. Who can sufficiently praise the daylily, the hybridizer's dream and the gardener's joy, a plant not even available to gardeners in the years of my earliest enthusiasm. Then we knew only the species, the tawny naturalized roadside daylily, *Hemerocallis fulva,* and the old-fashioned fragrant lemon-lily of spring, *H. flava.* Now there are thousands of cultivars, not only yellows but pinks, reds, melon, and lavender shades, some approaching green, day and evening bloomers, dwarfs and giants. To suggest even a limited list of favorite cultivars is hardly possible. Even so, here is one, developed with anguish I am sure for the omissions, by my friend Edna Payne, who is a collector of the best. This dozen includes the most popular of fairly new cultivars. And daylilies are not demanding. They prefer a well-drained location and rather shallow planting, only an inch or so of soil covering the crowns. I sprinkle superphosphate around them in spring along with my potash-rich wood ashes. When plants are in heavy bud and bloom, I water deeply, for drought then is harmful.

Under the outer shade of a
great tree where the sun
pauses briefly in the
morning, daylilies like this
'Evelyn Claar' bloom
profusely through July.
GEORGE TALOUMIS PHOTO

DAYLILIES FOR TODAY

E—Early, June 1 to June 15; EM—Early Midseason, June 15 to July 1; M—Midseason, July 1 to Aug. 1; L—Late, Aug. 1 to Sept. 1

Variety	Color	Height	Season
Cartwheels	Gold	24″	M
Exalted Ruler	Coral-pink	32″	M
Full Reward	Cadmium Yellow	36″	EM
Hortensia	Medium Yellow	34″	M
Last Hurrah	Melon	25–28″	L
Lavender Flight	Lavender	24″	M
Love-That-Pink	Light Pink	26–28″	EM
Raspberry Cream	Bright Raspberry	24″	EM
Sweet Harmony	Pinkish Buff	32″	M
'Tis Midnight	Dark Maroon	32″	EM
Winning Ways	Greenish Yellow	32–34″	EM
Winsome Lady	Blush Pink	24″	E

Hostas

I once saw a place planted predominantly with hostas. It was a site with a number of rocky outcroppings and heavily shaded. The owners wanted low-upkeep plants but with some grace, and for them a number of different hostas, judiciously placed, was exactly right. Today some gardeners collect hostas, so rewarding are these low-upkeep shade-loving perennials. Their foliage varies from pale to deep green to blue-green; some have white markings that are as decorative as bloom in deep shade; some giants grow to 6 feet, some

Lovely in flower and leaf, hostas are among the best of the shade-preference perennials and alone can make a garden, so varied are their heights and forms. This handsome *Hosta tardiflora* opens pale lavender flowers in September. CHARLES MARDEN FITCH PHOTO

dwarfs to one. It would be easy for an enthusiast to assemble close to two dozen kinds, including some of the newer hybrids.

Hostas are also self-sufficient plants, staying healthy without spraying; even the tall ones require no stakes. Small varieties make a good groundcover for an extensive site, nice accents or edgings for the small garden. I don't think most of them mix well. Once I made a small grouping of the yellow-green-foliaged August-lily, *H. subcordata grandiflora,* with the blue-leaved *H. sieboldiana,* and I can't say I liked the effect, but I did enjoy the white one alone under a dogwood tree as a "hedge" for the Round Garden, where at a little distance from it the 12-inch white-bordered *H.* 'Minor Alba' made a pretty edging.

Other white-marked hostas, 'Thomas Hogg', 'Variegata', and 'Albo Marginata', are effective contrast plants in all-green settings, and you may like those with yellow markings like *H. fortunei* 'Aurea marmorata'. Except for the fragrant, white evening flowers of the old-fashioned, 2-foot August-lily that grows with ferns and laurel by the terrace steps, I've never been enraptured by the lavender or white blooms of the others; still, any florescence in *deep* shade is acceptable, I suppose.

The botanical names of hostas alarm me as much as those of ferns, and furthermore there is considerable confusion. I have tended to follow names and descriptions in catalogues since most of us obtain our plants from growers. When you order, read carefully the notes on heights and colors, and the leaf descriptions. Small hostas are hard to find and it may be that the little one I favor as 'Minor Alba' is also called 'Louisa'. (Oh, my!)

Anyway, hostas are really great shade plants, not particular as to soil but needing water in periods of dry weather. Space them well for they are exuberant growers that shouldn't need transplanting for years and years. The variegated types will have more pronounced markings in light than in deep shade. (See Color Section.)

FOR AUTUMN COLOR

In shade, you have to forego chrysanthemums, unless you enjoy them the way I do. I buy well-budded pot plants and set them in light shade *on top of the soil* in my shrub and perennial borders and on the entrance steps. Chrysanthemums grown from start-to-finish in the shade just aren't going to amount to anything. However, for fall, there are three other excellent flowering perennials, hardy ageratum, aconites, and anemones.

Hardy ageratum or mistflower, *Eupatorium coelestinum,* could never be called a refined grower. A nice, 2-foot lavender-flowering native, spreading rapidly, it has its uses if you have space for it and want something showy to cut for late summer into autumn. I like it to round out the season and to use in arrangements with chrysanthemums.

The aconites I've grown are the deep blue *Aconitum fischeri* (now called *A. carmichaelii,* for goodness' sake!), growing 2 to 3 feet high, and 'Sparks Variety', a little taller and later, both for light shade and to carry color well into September.

The windflower, *Anemone japonica,* is beautiful with delicate-looking flowers for fall. Blooming pink or white in abundance, on 2- to 3-foot plants in light shade and continuing to frost, anemones are welcome end-of-season plants. I particularly like the silvery pink 'September Charm'.

Then it's time, I think, that we became aware again, as were our grandmothers, of the garden value of strong clumps of the ornamental grasses. Catalogues are beginning to list a number of these. Particularly recommended for shady locations are the sea-oats, *Uniola latifolia,* and bottlebrush grass, *Hystrix patula.* Growing to 4 feet, both have showy late-summer and autumn flowers, and make good, fair-sized accent plants.

Now, look, you aren't possibly going to want some of all these grand possibilities for your lightly shaded areas. Emphasize a few for each season and you will get the best effect and the most satisfaction.

Less valuable than the dominant three, but a pleasure to me, has been the tall ill-named snakeroot, *Cimicifuga simplex,* thriving with white wands in abundance where the soil is deep and rich. I grow it near the brook against the gray stone wall. It needs setting off with hemlocks perhaps, and you might enjoy this native evergreen as background in your wild garden. (See Color Section.)

There too you might like a clump of that favorite of mine, the fragrant, blush-white garden heliotrope, *Valeriana officinalis,* but I have this under the apple tree. It seeds itself readily and has also made a fine stand next to one of the compost heaps.

Holding well into fall are two rather coarse growers that have possibilities where you have space for them and want summer-into-fall color. The globe-thistle, particularly 'Taplow Blue', to 3 feet, covers a stretch at one side of a short flight of steps here. However, it need not be among your essentials unless you need it for drying, for it has excellent form for dried bouquets and will supply you with cut flowers well into September. Beebalm, *Monarda didyma,* blooms into August, preferably in moist woodland though it has thrived elsewhere for me in light shade. It is nice to cut and to dry, and a favorite of hummingbirds. Daisies as a whole require full sun but the enduring cutleaf coneflower, *Rudbeckia speciosa,* blooms well in half-shade. It's rather coarse but has its uses and dries beautifully. Other gardeners report August to October bloom from *R.* 'Goldsturm' in a damp shady border.

CHOICE PERENNIALS FOR SHADED PLACES

All will flourish in the light of high-pruned trees. Some will tolerate somewhat deeper shade as I have indicated. Select these if not much sunlight comes through your trees.

Name	Height	Description	Culture	Remarks
Aconitum carmichaelii (*A. fischeri*) Aconite	2–3'	Purple helmet flowers, Aug.–Sept., may grow taller, depends on conditions; good foliage.	Light shade, rich soil, doesn't care for moving about or drought.	Nice with anemones; 'Sparks Variety' 3–4', darker blue, blooms well into Sept.
Alkanet, see *Anchusa*				
Anchusa azurea Alkanet, Bugloss	3–5'	Lovely bright-blue panicles for June–July.	Half to light shade, don't let seed form, needs good drainage, likes some lime.	Good tall blue instead of delphinium for shaded borders; 'Dropmore' deep blue.
Anemone japonica Windflower	2–3'	Rose, white, single or double, Sept.–Oct.	Half to light shade.	Among best for early autumn in garden or to cut. 'September Charm' lovely silvery pink.

pulsatilla Pasqueflower	9–12"	Purple, golden anthers, Apr.–May.		Enchanting species for edging; along rocky steps, lasting feathery foliage.
vitifolia	30"	Pink, Aug.–Oct.		Similar to *A. japonica* but hardier, withstanding severe winters; spreads rapidly.
Aquilegia caerulea Colorado Columbine	30"	Lavender, May–June, native.	Light shade.	Rocky Mountain columbine, dainty, airy plants.
chrysantha	30"	Yellow, May–July, native.		Bushy, floriferous species.
flabellata nana	6–8"	White, blue-gray foliage.		Dwarf for edging.
McKana Hybrids	30"	Pink, purple, red, yellow, white, May–July.		Large, long-spurred blooms, lovely flowers to cut.
Arabis alpina (albida) Rockcress	6"	April–May.	Light shade.	Keep tidy by pruning back straggling growth; pretty edger, especially nice with violas in rock garden; not always reliable.

Name	Height	Description	Culture	Remarks
Aster x frikartii	1½–2′	Large, single lavender flowers, late June to frost.	Light shade.	'Wonder of Staffa' is the aster I have grown best in shade, but some dwarf and semidwarf types would be worth trying for early autumn color.
Aster novi-belgii New York Aster	3′	Bright-violet flowers, Sept.–Oct., native.	Half-shade and moisture.	Feathery and lovely for fall.
Astilbe, Hybrids	18″–4′	White, pink, red, June–Aug.	Light to quite deep shade; rich moist soil, must not get dry.	Marvelous pestfree plants, dependable bloomers, enduring foliage, my first choice for shade. Fine to cut: split stems as you do shrubs. Dry flowers for winter bouquets.
August-lily, see *Hosta*				
Balloon-flower, see *Platycodon*				

Baptisia australis	2–3'	Blue, pea-shaped flowers in June, native.	Light shade.	Lasting foliage, good blue for center border accent; needs plenty of space, to 18" or more.
Beebalm, Bergamot, see *Monarda*				
Bergenia cordifolia	12–20"	Pink or white spikes, May.	Open to deep shade, moist to wet soil.	Handsome dark green fleshy rosettes of foliage; impressive, good for forefront of shrubs, making large clumps.
Bleedingheart, see *Dicentra*				
Bluebell, see *Campanula*				
Bottlebrush-grass, see *Hystrix*				
Brunnera macrophylla (*Anchusa myosotidiflora*)	18"	Blue, May–June.	Open shade to sun, deep moist soil.	Fine true-blue forget-me-not flowers; large spreading plants, coarse leaves. (Woodchucks ate mine.)
Bugloss, see *Anchusa*				

Name	Height	Description	Culture	Remarks
Campanula carpatica Carpathian Bluebell	8–10"	Blue, white, June–Oct.	Light shade, good drainage.	For rock garden or border, nice edger; enduring leaves.
persicifolia Peachbells	2'	June, reblooms if stems cut back.		Taller for mid-border; also good white.
Candytuft, see *Iberis*				
Ceratostigma plumbaginoides (*Plumbago larpentae*) Leadwort, Plumbago	6"	Dark blue, Aug.–Sept.	Part shade or sun.	Not the greatest, though color is good. (Terrible new name!)
Cowslip, see *Primula*				
Daylily, see *Hemerocallis*				
Delphinium grandiflorum (*chinese*) Chinese Delphinium	3–4'	Blue, white, late June–July.	Open to sky, bloomed satisfactorily without sun here. Best to treat as biennial.	Intermittent bloom; cut back between bursts; iffy in shade, worth trying.
Coralbells, see *Heuchera sanguinea*				If you want delphiniums; good blue for cutting. (Species seed hard to find.)

Dicentra eximia Plumy Bleedingheart	1'	Pink, May–Oct., native.	Shade or sun.	Ferny, persistent foliage, good groundcover.
spectabilis Common Bleedingheart	2'	Pink, May–June.	Light open shade.	Handsome but summer disappearance; even so, indispensable plant with ferns for a cover-up.
Dictamnus albus Gasplant	3'	White also pink and purple varieties showy racemes in June; good foliage.	Open shade, rich loam, well-drained soil; avoid transplanting.	Generally recommended for full sun but performs handsomely for me in apple-tree shade; flowers can be ignited without danger to plant.
Digitalis ambigua Foxglove	30"	Yellow tubular flowers, June–July; true perennial.	Shade, moisture.	This flourished for me in fairly deep shade next to a stone wall, lovely I thought. Newer biennial Hyacinth Hybrids white-to-rose shades.
Doronicum Hybrids Leopardbane	12–18"	Yellow, April–May.	Open shade.	Good spring yellow; dormant in summer. Lovely with bleedinghearts and mertensia.

Name	Height	Description	Culture	Remarks
Echinops exaltatus Globe-thistle	3–4'	Purple, July–Sept.	Light shade.	Coarse grower, very hardy, good for dried bouquets; 'Taplow Blue' best.
Epimedium, see Groundcover and Wildflower Charts (Don't miss this!)				
Eupatorium coelestinum Hardy Ageratum	2–3'	Lavender flowers, Aug.–Oct., native.	Light shade, moisture.	Weedy grower; plant where you want coverage. Useful fall color with chrysanthemums; nice to cut, good in wild garden.
Evening-primrose, see *Oenothera*				
Filipendula vulgaris (*hexapetala*) Meadowsweet	18"	Pink in bud, white clusters, double flowers held on straight stems above low ferny rosettes, July–Aug.	Light shade.	Good cut flower; needs moisture; I planted it in woodland.

Foxglove, see *Digitalis*				
Garden Heliotrope, see *Valeriana*				
Gasplant, see *Dictamnus*				
Globeflower, see *Trollius*				
Hardy Ageratum, see *Eupatorium*				
Helleborus niger Christmas-rose	1′	Pink-white, Jan.–Feb.; later in some years, depending on weather.	Light to deeper shade; doesn't care for moving about; avoid drought in summer.	Evergreen foliage; choice and essential. The Lenten rose, *H. orientalis*, dark purple, grows in fern garden; rather dull plant.
Hemerocallis Daylily	1½–4′	Cream, green, pink, yellow, orange, May–Sept. Some 8,000 hybrids, marvelous gamut of heights and coloring.	Light to fairly deep shade; best bloom in full light or sun.	For woodland with ferns, species *H. flava*, *H. fulva* more appropriate than garden hybrids, although I do enjoy a few hybrids in my woodland. Summer essentials.

Name	Height	Description	Culture	Remarks
Heuchera sanguinea Coralbells	12–18″	Rose, scarlet, white, June–Aug.	Very light shade.	Excellent for edging here, gets some early sunshine.
Hosta (Funkia) Plantain-lily	1–3′	White, lavender, purple flowers, July–Sept., handsome foliage, green, blue-green, variegated.	Light shade, ordinary garden soil but be sure to keep well watered.	August-lily *H. subcordata grandiflora* to 2′, white, fragrant, a favorite here, many fine newer hybrids; low types good groundcover.
Hystrix patula Bottlebrush-grass	4′	Ornamental grass, showy white spikes of bloom late summer.	Light to deep shade.	Interesting accent plant with a difference; other ornamental grasses worth trying.
Iberis sempervirens Hardy Candytuft	12″	White, Apr.–June.	Shade or sun; excellent for a sun-to-shade border.	Sprawling evergreen species, my favorite edging plant; requires winter antidesiccant protection if in sun, not in shade.

	Height	Color / Bloom	Light	Remarks
'Autumn Snow'	6"	White, Apr.–May; may repeat.		Three varieties neat and compact; fine for formal edging. 'Purity' a little larger than the others; all evergreen.
'Little Gem'	6"	White, May.		
'Purity'	6"	White, May.		
Iris cristata Crested Iris	3–4"	Pale lavender, white, May–June, native.	Partial shade required.	Can be used as groundcover, choice.
kaempferi Japanese Iris	2–3"	Pink, purple, white, June–July.	Shade; moisture but not for bogs.	Handsome flat blooms along brook where open to sky; lovely with royal ferns.
gracilipes Slender Iris	8–10"	Pinkish-lilac or white, May, grassy foliage.	Light shade. Loose leaf soil.	Nice for rock garden or woodland, but hard to find.
pseudacorus Yellow Flag	3'	Yellow, May–June.	Light shade.	White to yellow, a volunteer here along brook, excellent for wet places.
sibirica Siberian Iris	2–3"	Purple, white, grassy foliage, June.	Light shade, deep planting, dependable.	For accent clumps or in wide borders; blue 'Gatineau', very dark 'Caesar's Brother', 'Snowcrest' all good.

Name	Height	Description	Culture	Remarks
Iris continued *tectorum* Roof Iris	1'	White or purple, May.	Light shade.	Under Christmas-berry-tree with early daffodils and crocus.
versicolor Blue Flag	1'	Purple, June–July, native.	Shade, bogs.	Wild blue flag with small flowers, volunteered along brook; often naturalizes, good in moist soil.
Leadwort, see *Ceratostigma*				
Leopardbane, see *Doronicum*				
Meadowrue, see *Thalictrum*				
Meadowsweet, see *Filipendula*				
Mertensia virginica, see Wildflower Chart Virginia Bluebells				
Monarda didyma Beebalm, Bergamot	36"	Pink, red, lavender, white, July, native.	Open shade.	Fast spreader, good background border plant or as here in open woods, also for dried bouquets.

Oenothera fruticosa Evening-primrose	1½–2′	Yellow, June–July.	Light shade or sun; dry soil.	Showy and spreading, good groundcover. Nice under *Lilium tigrinum*.
Paeonia albiflora hybrids Peony	2–3′	Red, pink, white, single, double, late May–June.	Here in light shade with a few hours of morning sun.	Familiar garden peony.
suffruticosa (*Moutan*) and *lutea* Tree Peony	3–4′	Same colors, also yellow, mid-May–June.	Light shade.	Shrubby tree peony; don't cut back; good here under hawthorn.
Peony, see *Paeonia*				
Physostegia virginiana False Dragonhead	18–36″	Pink, white, lavender, July–Sept, native.	Light open shade.	Coarse, spreading; reliable but best kept out of controlled plantings; tried to take over the Apple-tree Garden.
Plantain-lily, see *Hosta*				
Platycodon grandiflorum Balloon-flower	18–24″	Purple, white, June–Oct.	Fairly deep shade here under silverbell-tree.	Fine foliage, appears late, good concealer for bulbs.

Name	Height	Description	Culture	Remarks
Plumbago, see *Ceratostigma*				
Primula, see Wildflower Chart Cowslip, Primrose				
Rockcress, see *Arabis*				
Rudbeckia species and hybrids Coneflower	2–3'	Red, yellow, white, July on, native.	Part shade.	Not the most refined but carefree and showy "daisy" plants for late summer, as 'Gold Drop', 'White Luster', etc. but not droopy species. 'Goldsturm' blooms Aug.–Oct. in a damp border; all good flowers for drying.
Sea-oats, see *Uniola*				
Trollius europaeus Globeflower	2'	Yellow, orange, May–July.	Partial shade; also good in sun.	Buttercup blooms, charming in spring groupings, good lasting foliage.

Thermopsis caroliniana Carolina-lupine	3–4'	Yellow pealike flowers in spikes, June–July.	Light shade.	Good accent plant, too little grown, charming.
Tufted Pansy, see *Viola*				
Uniola latifolia Sea-oats	4'	Ornamental grass, arching clumps, showy for late-summer bloom.	Light to deep shade.	Rich autumn tints; good garden accent.
Valeriana officinalis Garden Heliotrope	30–36"	Blush-white, June–July.	Light shade.	Heliotrope scent, blooms under apple tree; has also seeded next compost heaps.
Viola cornuta Tufted Pansy (See also Wildflower Chart)	6"	Yellow, white, purple, apricot, Apr.–Oct., good scent in some.	Light shade.	Charming small perennial pansy, not always heat-resistant, needs winter protection.
odorata Sweet Violet	8"	Purple, Apr.–May; repeats in fall.	Rich soil and moisture.	Fine fragrance; 'Royal Robe' and 'White Czar' lovely cultivars.
Windflower, see *Anemone*				

White impatiens blooms freely in this brick-edged bed under the fairly heavy shade of an ancient crab-apple tree. This annual now comes in many colors and various sizes, one of the very best for bloom in shade. GEORGE TALOUMIS PHOTO

ANNUALS THAT PREFER
OR TOLERATE SHADE

Just a Matter of Selection

If your marigolds and zinnias have been a disappointment, don't think you must forego annuals because your place is shady. There are annuals that absolutely require shade, and quite a number that perform well where there is full light but no sun or in a half-and-half situation where two or three hours of sunshine reach them.

The Two Best

Two absolutely dependable treasures are impatiens and wax begonias. Both flower freely all summer here in light shade and open north light. Potted up in August, they bloom all winter, too. Under my four-pronged white birch tree with Christmas ferns and evergreen hellebores, the pastel impatiens looks lovely. It also comes ir deeper colors—red, salmon, coral, and orange—as well as a pleasing lavender. The Elfin series grows to 6 inches, the Imps to 15 inches, taller hybrids to 2 feet, and you can have doubles if you wish.

Growing plants from seed that need 8 to 10 weeks from sowing to outdoors is much too much bother for me so I buy my impatiens and other long-do annuals in bud at a roadside stand or nursery. If you buy plants, watch out that they have not been allowed to dry out (they usually recover but it takes time) or to develop spindly growth. Select the impatiens that suits your purpose for color and plant height. In some years I have matched impatiens color with petunias at the edge of a bed where there is a little sunlight. Thus 'Elfin Salmon' impatiens and coral 'Magic' petunias are a pretty pair. Recently I tried a strong contrast in impatiens and liked it— an orange Imp with Park's 'Snowflake'. The bright effect was exactly right in a rather dark place. Then there is a strain called Shady Lady Pastel Colors, in blush to rose; for a garden emphasizing soft colors, these would be nice.

Today hybridizers aware of our need for bloom in shade are doing great things with impatiens. Park's and Burpee's catalogues list and illustrate many new ones you will enjoy. I can't say that I like the bicolors or those with dark leaves, but to each his own, of course. And in fall when you are bulb planting, give thought to "circle setting," a ring of bulbs where you can fill in the center with impatiens or other spreading annuals early enough for the developing plants to hide the maturing bulb foliage.

Impatiens balsamina, garden-balsam or touch-me-not, also thrives in shade. I have known it as a rather stiff upright grower to 3 feet with flowers like camellias straight up the stems. For a narrow space between house wall and walk, this is a good choice, but you may have to grow it from seed, for I haven't seen any started plants for sale. 'Princess Sakura' is a lovely tall red-marked pink. Today you can also grow a bush-flowered dwarf type, but for low plants I prefer the other impatiens.

The wax begonia (*B. semperflorens*) is colorful and equally prolific. Concealing the departing hyacinths and daffodils, these flourish in the once sunny bed under the kitchen casements, an area where little sun now shines because of the low shade of nearby shrubs. Elsewhere begonias are bedding plants before a pair of espaliered *Viburnum carlesii.* They make lusty summer growth with pure white, rose, or red single or double flowers, the male flowers with fluffy golden centers. Some have green foliage, like the Cinderella Strain and 'Butterfly', with 3-inch flowers; some, like the new 'Danica', have coppery leaves. Begonia colors blend well; don't be afraid to grow mixtures, and do plan to pot up some plants in August for continued winter bloom. (See Color Section.)

True Blues and Violet

Although violet shades abound, there are few really blue garden flowers, except for delphiniums, which are, of course, sun-demanding. For our shaded sites, there is baby-blue-eyes, *Nemophila insignis,* not important but still a pretty 6-inch edger or groundcover for bulbs. Sow outdoors in April or in fall where it can stay; it will open cup-shaped flowers from June to frost.

The Chinese forget-me-not, *Cynoglossum amabile,* also blooms from June on if sown indoors in March, outdoors early in May. It is tall enough, 18 to 24 inches, to carry true blue through a border, but will not flourish without *some* sun; best to use it in half-and-half locations.

The true forget-me-nots make a lovely underplanting for bulbs, and I always enjoy the blue wave that carpets the apple-tree planting of bleedinghearts and the perennial blue mertensia. Goodnamed forget-me-nots are 'Blue Bird', a light shade, and 'Royal Blue' a deeper color. Whether listed as annual or biennial, they selfsow most satisfactorily and, if you let them go to seed—they do look shabby for a couple of weeks—they will provide you with a permanent stand. The new little plants are easy to move and can be set all over the garden for next spring's loveliness. You may also find them, as I have, in odd places some distance away, the seeds having fallen into the crevices of a flagstone path or under a big daylily.

Dependable and choice is the annual lobelia, *L. erinus*. Bedding varieties with compact growth like 'Cambridge Blue' make a charming edging; the trailers or Cascade types are perfect for window boxes or hanging baskets. One summer I fastened one of those half-round containers of 'Blue Cascade' against the white wall of the house at the front door. It was a pleasant sight as I went in or came out. There are also fine violet-shaded lobelias, like the compact 'Bright Eyes' (this one always looks mischievous to me), and trailing 'Sapphire'. A friend planted a hanging basket of this one with a pink tuberous begonia. Suspended against a redwood wall, in half not deep shade (the begonia doesn't care for too dim a spot), the basket was colorful from June to frost. There are also trailing red lobelias, nice to combine with white wax begonias in a somewhat shaded window box.

Browallia with bell-like flowers up to 2 inches tends to lavender and purple although 'Powder Blue' is lighter and bluer. It makes a nice pot plant for the terrace (or window) or edging a garden bed that runs from sun to shade. It needs a long growing period, so for early color outdoors you might sow this one indoors in March. I enjoy it as a bedding plant that brings summer color to an area after the spring bulbs have gone.

The flossflower, *Ageratum,* is one of the most dependable of all edging plants, shade to sun, and readily available as well-started plants. The 4-inch midget types bring good color to a narrow bed, but there are tall growers for long-lasting cut flowers and the shaded garden hardly produces enough of such. You can have ageratums in other than the familiar lavender or purple shades, as 'Summer Snow' and 'Fairy Pink', a good salmon shade.

White for Evening Pleasure

I can't remember when I didn't grow sweet alyssum, now called *Lobularia maritima*. It flourishes in shade or sun, and can be purchased as blooming plants, but why? Seed sown outdoors early in April where plants are to bloom produces flowers of honeycomb

The white-flowering tobacco, *Nicotiana affinis,* blooms in full light, more freely in half-and-half shade with a little sunshine through part of the day.

GEORGE TALMOUIS PHOTO

scent from May to frost or a little beyond, for the plants are cold-hardy, and the fragrance is pleasantly sharp in the cold days of early autumn. Shear the plants a little to keep them tidy. The spreading 'Carpet of Snow' will need this attention more than the compact 'Little Gem' or purple 'Royal Carpet'. But Carpet is my favorite; I have a nostalgic affection for it. Once on a train journey to California I made a new friend. Comparing garden notes, we discovered that we both depended for edgings on Dreer's "1101" packets of 'Carpet of Snow'. Dreer's is long since out of business but the Carpet still pleases and is choice for the evening garden where white flowers are best.

Flowering tobacco, *Nicotiana,* long a night-blooming favorite for its marvelously sweet after-dark fragrance, is now available in varieties that stay open through the day. 'White Bedder', a dwarf to 12 inches, and 'Lime Sherbet', a creamy chartreuse, to 18 inches, are good choices. However, I have found it best to assure these full light and a little sun if possible. In a northern situation, too heavily shaded by the apple tree, they were disappointing for me.

Other Possibilities

The number of annuals that will bloom satisfactorily in the shade, some not so luxuriantly as in sun perhaps, is considerable. To have variety beyond the completely reliable impatiens and wax begonias, you have to experiment, trying one or more different ones under your own conditions each year. Seedsmen, realizing our need for flowers in shade, are now listing shade groups in their catalogues. Recommended by some writers are nasturtiums and heliotrope. These I can't imagine being successful, but I may be wrong, and there are various others worth a try.

As for petunias, they must have *some* sunlight, but have prospered for me in a half-and-half location. The small-flowered kinds require less sun than the big ones.

Flower arrangers can get a good reseeding crop of green bells-of-Ireland with April-sown seed, and then they have flowers to dry in the fall. The annual vinca in white, or rose-centered white, or pink looks rather like a begonia with its glossy green foliage; it is notably reliable in shade. I have enjoyed violas, too. These have performed as hardy annuals if I cut them back at the start of very hot weather and dose them heavily with a soluble fertilizer late in August. In this way both spring and fall crops are assured, with overwintering if I tuck pine needles under the green tops. Of all violas, 'Yellow Perfection' and 'Apricot' are my favorites. I once had a delightful grouping of 'Apricot' with the perennial white rockcress under a hickory tree.

Perhaps you will want to grow the Pastel Strain of *Salvia splendens*. This brings color to a dim area, and for my money has it all over the familiar scarlet sage. Maybe the wishbone-flower,

In light shade and open north light, pink impatiens (following the spring bulbs) is a colorful sight from spring to frost under my four-pronged white birch tree with Christmas ferns and Christmas-roses in the deeper shade at the back. GEORGE TALOUMIS PHOTO

Torenia, will appeal or the monkey-flower, *Mimulus.* Whatever you select from the marvelous possibilities, do include some coleus. The leaves, strikingly colored and patterned, are as effective as flowers. Coleus comes tall or dwarf, in green and white or cream, or in mixtures bright as an Indian blanket. The Carefree Strain—jade, yellow, red, and in muted tones—is easy and attractive. My own best favorite is 'Firebird'. It lights up the garden all summer, a south window all winter; and cuttings make a pretty breakfast-table bouquet. (See Color Section.)

ANNUALS FOR COLOR IN THE SHADE

Planted in areas open to the sky or in half-shade, most of these will be satisfactory; in general, annuals need some sun except as indicated here. The edge of a shaded border where the sun strikes for 2 or 3 hours is a good place for most of them.

Name	Height in Inches	Description	Culture	Remarks
Ageratum Flossflower	3–24	Small, fluffy lavender, pink, or white blooms.	Allow 3 months indoors from seed, or buy started plants.	Dwarf types most useful for shade-to-sun edgings, and good indoor pot plants.
Antirrhinum majus hybrids Snapdragon	8–36	All colors but blue; types for bedding; dwarfs and giants.	Sow indoors 6 weeks ahead of outdoor planting or outdoors when soil is warm; transplant 12 to 18″ apart.	Fine cut flower worth trying; reports of good bloom in light shade.
Baby-blue-eyes, see *Nemophila*				

Name	Height in Inches	Description	Culture	Remarks
Begonia semperflorens Wax Begonia	6–12	Clusters of pink, white, red flowers with more or less prominent fluffy yellow centers; green or bronze foliage.	Useful for full light or morning sun, afternoon shade.	With impatiens, this is one of the most reliable of all flowering annuals for shade; neat grower discarding faded flowers readily; pot up for bloom all winter, too.
Bells-of-Ireland, see *Molucella*				
Browallia speciosa	8–10	Mainly violet shades, blooms June to frost.	Sow indoors early Mar. or outdoors in May.	After a showy summer outdoors, this also makes a fine winter window plant. 'Powder Blue' nearer true-blue shade.
Chinese Forget-me-not, see *Cynoglossum*				

Coleus blumei	12–24	Fine foliage color, chartreuse to scarlet; new dwarf Carefree Strain very handsome.	Sow indoors 12 weeks before last frost, or buy well-started plants. Cut off flowers; they are not attractive.	Foliage brings color to dim places, also good pot plant for terrace and window garden, smaller types good for window boxes in shade.
Cynoglossum amabile Chinese Forget-me-not	18–24	Lovely clear blue, June on.	Sow indoors in Mar., outdoors in May, half-and-half shade, not deep.	Carries true blue through center of shaded border.
Flossflower, see *Ageratum*				
Flowering Tobacco, see *Nicotiana*				
Forget-me-not, see *Myosotis*				
Garden Balsam, see *Impatiens*				

Name	Height in Inches	Description	Culture	Remarks
Impatiens balsamina Garden Balsam Touch-me-not	12–36	Single and double flowers, some resembling camellias, white, red, purple.	Blooms 8–10 weeks from seed, needs rich soil.	Good color in shade, emphatic not graceful grower, also good for winter flowers.
walleriana (sultanii) Patience-plant Patient Lucy	6–24	White, pink, red, lavender, orange; see Park's catalogue for varieties.	Sow Feb. for garden in May, or buy-in-bud plants; blooms to frost. Space 18″ apart.	Absolutely the best annual for heavy bloom in light to deep shade; pot in fall for all-winter bloom.
Lobelia erinus	4–9	White, pink, blue, red, June to frost; compact bedding and cascade types.	May live over winter if mulched.	Good sun-to-shade edging for a long border, or trailer for hanging basket or window box in light shade. Also good indoor pot plant.
Lobularia maritima Sweet Alyssum	3–10	White, purple; pretty, fragrant edging plant.	Sow outdoors early Apr. for May-to-frost flowers; shear sprawly growth to promote bloom.	Marvelous honey fragrance; 'Carpet of Snow' spreading, 'Little Gem', compact, both white; purple 'Royal Carpet' only 3–4″. Pot some for house plants.

Mimulus tigrinus (*cupreus*) Monkey- (not tiger!) flower	4–12	Red, yellow; summer to frost.	Sow indoors in Mar.	Not the greatest but a useful color in shade.
Molucella laevis Bells-of-Ireland	24	Large bracted calyx gives effect of green "flower."	Sow outdoors Apr. in permanent place and let reseed for future crops.	Flower arrangers' delight, good for drying.
Monkey-flower, see *Mimulus*				
Myosotis sylvatica Forget-me-not	6–12	Blue, pink, white, in summer.	Not so moisture-dependent as perennial kinds.	Annual or biennial, these readily selfsow and stay with you forever if you are patient; let them go to seed each year.
Nemophila insignis Baby-blue-eyes	6	Blue, June to frost; lovely color.	Sow outdoors in Apr. for long season, or outdoors in fall for early spring.	Nice edger or groundcover for bulbs; pretty, not vital.

Name	Height in Inches	Description	Culture	Remarks
Nicotiana Flowering Tobacco	12–18	White, chartreuse, rose, dark red. Blooms all summer.	No frost endurance; open shade essential, some sun advisable.	'White Bedder', 'Dwarf White Bedder', and 'Lime Sherbet' have fine fragrance, stay open both day and evening; good night-garden flowers.
Pansy, see *Viola*				
Patience-plant, see *Impatiens*				
Periwinkle, see *Vinca*				
Petunia	10–24	White, pink, purple, red, near yellow.	Endures half-shade, otherwise iffy. Sow early indoors or buy plants; dwarf types now available.	Small-flowering kinds best to try; planted at edge of shaded border with some afternoon sun satisfactory here.
Salvia splendens: Pastel Strain	6–24	White, purple, pink.	Sow seeds indoors in Feb.	New strain worth trying in the shade.

Snapdragon, see *Antirrhinum*				
Sweet Alyssum, see *Lobularia*				
Torenia fournieri Wishbone-flower	12	White, yellow, purple, June to frost.	Rather moist soil. Set young plants 8" apart.	Pot some plants for window garden bloom through winter.
Touch-me-not, see *Impatiens*				
Vinca rosea Periwinkle	15 or trailing	White, pink, white with a rosy eye.	Endures almost any conditions of soil and location.	Try this; it looks delicate but isn't; nice for bedding or a window box.
Viola tricolor Pansy	8	Purple shades, yellow, white, garnet. Buy plants.	Likes it cool, best bloom spring and fall.	Cut well back after heavy spring bloom and fertilize for fall flowers; often winters over, here.
Wax Begonia, see *Begonia*				
Wishbone-flower, see *Torenia*				

The indispensable evergreen mountain-laurel, *Kalmia latifolia,* with pink-white shell-like flowers in June, blooms here in an open northerly location that is in full light but not sunny. GEORGE TALOUMIS PHOTO

9

FLOWERING, FRUITING, AND EVERGREEN SHRUBS

For Color and Backgrounds

When it comes to shrubs, shade gardening is at its most rewarding. In fact, the owner of a sunstruck place visiting your cool and shadowed garden on a hot day and seeing your wealth of bloom may well go home determined to plant and plant until the pleasures—and opportunities—of shade can replace the supposedly broader scope of open heat.

Azaleas for Pageantry

Rhododendrons, especially azaleas, which are included in the genus, are among the most colorful flowering shrubs in shade. With these you can enjoy a spring-to-summer pageant of species and hybrids, and support the picture with such spring-flowering broadleafs as the two andromedas and leucothoe, which also bloom in shade. Many other shrubs will bring you flowers for every season, fine autumn color, and great crops of berries to attract the birds.

Because azaleas have so delighted me, I want to discuss first the deciduous species that bloom so gloriously in sequence from late April to July in the Fern Garden. Since several azaleas are native to our Eastern woodlands from Maine to Florida, they are readily at home in gardens here. Others come to us from northeastern Asia where the climate is similar to much of ours in North America.

Azaleas require an acid humusy soil, cool moisture, and protection from wind. They will tolerate morning sun, and I have flourishing plantings that get several hours in a southern location under a white birch and a wild cherry tree. But azaleas also thrive in light shade or shifting sunlight under tall oaks, open pines, and lacy honeylocusts. I mulch the shallow roots with pine needles or decaying oak leaves; in a more formal setting the pine bark that comes in bags would look nice. I use a groundcover of pachysandra but don't let it get so close to plants it chokes them. Deep watering is essential through those weeks of drought that seem to hit here in August, occasionally for a spell in June. Azaleas don't care for dryness or extreme heat so the overhead sprinkler is put in play when the temperature soars.

If you have a woodland area, suitably thinned out, the trees high pruned, I am sure you will enjoy these species that have flourished so handsomely for me. Earliest of all in mid-April comes the 6-foot rosy lavender Chinese azalea, *Rhododendron mucronulatum.* I grew it first in my Philadelphia garden under an oak tree along with pale yellow forsythias. The group was just inside a white picket fence along the sidewalk where passersby enjoyed the spring preview as much as I did.

Early in May—late April in some years—the 6-foot *R. nudiflorum,* the Pinxter bloom or wild honeysuckle of our New England woodland, blooms pink-to-white with just a faint scent.

The roseshell azalea, *R. roseum,* to 9 feet, as richly clove-scented as a carnation, opens about the same time, and if you can't have both you might prefer this because the perfume is much richer,

In mid-April the 6-foot Chinese azalea, *Rhododendron mucronulatum,* is covered with rosy lavender bloom before the leaves open. In my northern exposure in Philadelphia, it resisted late frosts and looked lovely with pale yellow forsythia.
CHARLES MARDEN FITCH
PHOTO

and it is extremely hardy. The pink-stamened, pink-to-pale crimson flowers are a little larger, and both azaleas bloom before their leaves appear, as indicated by the *nudiflorum* in the name of the first one.

One of the finest for mid-May is the very tall, to 15 feet in time, royal azalea, *R. schlippenbachii.* You just must have this glorious, large, pink-flowering beauty with the added attraction of fall foliage that rivals the brilliant sugar maple. Native to Korea and Japan, it thrives here exuberantly and will for you too, provided the soil has the required acidity. (Alas, I must admit no fragrance; in compensation, it tolerates deeper shade than most of the others.)

In the fairly heavy shade of a well-pruned apple tree, the early May azalea, 'Delaware Valley White', puts on a handsome show. (This and 'Palestrina' among best whites.) PAUL E. GENEREUX PHOTO

Another for mid-May, and notably hardy, is the 6- to 9-foot R. *vaseyii,* the pinkshell azalea, an American species also in bloom before it leaves out. Foliage in fall is a pleasing light red, and this one is a wise selection if you have an overly moist soil condition.

Early in June the brilliant, 9-foot flame azalea, R. *calendulaceum,* native from Pennsylvania southward but hardy in southern

New England, glows in my woods. The clove scent is pronounced in this one and the bloom varies from pale to dark and is weather-resistant. It holds good looks for some two weeks even in sunshine, in case you need a plant for a shade-to-sun transition.

Covered with white flowers, accented with rosy filaments in mid-June, the well-named sweet azalea, *R. arborescens,* treelike at 10 feet, is a handsome sight. Sometimes even taller, the swamp azalea, *R. viscosum,* white-flowering and very fragrant, thrives in moist soil in shade and, for me, ends the species pageant in July except for its fall raiment of bronze-orange foliage.

Hybrid Azaleas

Meanwhile, as I have had space, I have planted numerous azalea hybrids, both the evergreen or perhaps I should say semievergreen types, and the deciduous beauties. These glorify the border plantings through May and June associating charmingly with hemlocks, white birches, and ferns. Kurumes, Gables, and Glenn Dales tend to hold foliage through winter. Among these I like 'Blaauw's Pink' and 'Rosebud'; three whites, including 'Vestal', 'Palestrina', and 'Delaware Valley White', this last assuredly evergreen; and the charming white-shaded salmon-pink 'Ruth May', a hybrid introduced by the Olivers here in Connecticut.

Fine deciduous azaleas to grow in light or half-shade are legion. I seem to run to the yellow Ghents, the very fragrant 'Davisii', 'Nancy Waterer', and double 'Narcissiflora', but the Exburys, developed in England on the Rothschild estate, are gloriously tempting singles and doubles, pink, white, red, or orange. For a brilliant accent, there is the burnt-orange 'Gibraltar', for delicate beauty my favorite, the large-flowering yellow-touched white 'Toucan'. If you have a rock garden, the 8- to 10-inch lilac-flowered azalea, *R. kiusianum,* with miniature foliage will be charming.

All of these have proved hardy for me, though the evergreens incline to be semis. My place is in Zone 6 on the *U.S.D.A. Plant Hardiness Map,* and most of these azaleas are recommended for as far north as Zone 5. (See Color Section.)

Rhododendrons and Other Evergreens

Of the true rhododendrons, I have little to say. I have grown few of them; I suppose because I don't care much for them, especially the large-leaved types. They are highly recommended for winter effect but in frigid weather those curled up leaves give me a chill. However, I think the 5-foot, small-leaved Carolina rhododendron is lovely in mid-May when it is covered with rosy purple blooms. This one is said to be the first to roll its leaves at 20 degrees F. Three excellent hybrids—small-leaved, dwarf, and spreading— are the white 'Dora Amateis', blue-violet 'Ramapo', and soft pink 'Windbeam'. These make a graceful finish for foundation plantings, as does *R.* x *laetevirens,* the Wilson rhododendron, an evergreen hybrid to 4 feet with pink-to-purple flowers in early June. It is well suited for a prominent place in part-shade in a rock garden. The large-leaved lavender 'Blue Peter' and low-growing, pure white 'Boule de Neige' are much favored by landscape architects.

The flowering broadleafs that associate beautifully with azaleas and rhododendrons are also attractive grouped by themselves. Most of them perform well even in fairly deep shade, as I have grown them, and include the mountain-laurel. This blooms in an open northerly exposure, fully light but without sun. Truly, I cannot imagine a planted place without its choice pink-white shell-like flowers in June; perhaps it is my favorite flowering ever- green. The pendent white sprays of drooping leucothoe are in pleasing contrast, and the andromedas, upright or nodding and fragrant, are plants that bloom here in shaded northern locations along with the Japanese skimmia. With these I have planted the prickly Oregon holly-grape, neither holly nor grape but with fra- grant chartreuse blooms. Late in May the cherry-laurel is covered with white racemes to brighten a shaded evergreen planting.

Evergreens for Accent

More important for foliage than flowers are the barberries, box-
woods, cotoneasters, euonymus, privets, and hollies. These can be
planted for important green accents and some, especially little leaf
or dwarf box and the privets, used for hedges. None requires the
sun. Of the needle evergreens, the yews are invaluable. I have the
spreading type, *Taxus cuspidata* 'Densa', in quite deep shade between house and lawn. The columnar types are fine for corner
accents.

Then there are the tall and glorious hemlocks, of all evergreen
trees the most handsome. You can plant one as a mighty accent,
if you have plenty of room, or many as a *broad* hedge, the trees
sheared for density. I enjoy a dark hemlock associated with golden
forsythias for an early spring picture, and elsewhere green hemlocks
behind white birches for a lovely winter-long effect.

Of course, I hope you can have an American holly tree, quite
fast-growing here in this acid soil and protected from leaf miner
along with the birches. My tree rises above mountain-laurels beside the path to the Round Garden. Being a female tree, it fruits
heavily, a source of welcome Christmas decorations. A small male
tree, essential for pollination, is planted inconspicuously at the side
of the fern path.

For a Deciduous Border

In addition to azaleas, under high-pruned, deep-rooted trees, you
can enjoy a fine procession of deciduous flowering shrubs from
February to frost. And these offer so much for so little attention,
they will be particularly rewarding to you if your gardening time
is limited. In a border, say 6 to 8 feet deep, with a 12- to 18-inch
edge planted with spring bulbs, you could have a fine flowering
succession. Among the bulbs, as they fade, insert well-started

This Japanese *Pieris andromeda,* with handsome white braids of bloom in mid-April, its young foliage a glistening bronze, rises beside my northern dining-room window where the light is good.
CHARLES MARDEN FITCH PHOTO

plants you can buy of impatiens and wax begonias. Then, with the lowest possible upkeep, you will have a pleasing garden of early-to-late bloom.

Here is a possible sequence with an asterisk to indicate my seven suggestions. If your border is extensive, select more. The charts that follow this chapter will give you details and botanical names for ordering.

DECIDUOUS SHRUB SEQUENCE

February–March–early April

February Daphne
Vernal Witch-hazel
*Winter Honeysuckle, semievergreen;
    very fragrant
White-forsythia (so-called)

April–May

*Forsythia (true) 'Spring Glory'
*Pink Snowball
*Doublefile Viburnum
Flowering Quince
Deutzia
Lilacs (if *some* sun)
*Bridalwreath
Kerria
Tree Peony (some sun)
Mock-orange (species)

June–July

*Mock-orange 'Belle Etoile'
Hydrangeas
Buttercup-shrub (to October)

August–Frost

*Franklinia

Here I should add a note on lilacs. I must have them but lilacs bloom meagerly even in half-shade and, if they are at the edge of a shady border, they will bend out toward the sun and then hardly be shapely plants. However, the branches that get sun or sky shine will set buds and so my crowded plants have produced enough blooms, particularly at the top, for me to have some delectable flowers to cut.

Valuable Viburnums

In your border, include more viburnums if you can. At least six are reliable—I'd like to say indispensable—for fine flowering in shade. The 8-foot or taller pink snowball, *V. carlesii,* gives a striking performance because it blooms April–May before most trees leaf out. Espaliered against a southern house wall, heavily shaded later by a Christmas-berry-tree, it blooms richly and fragrantly, some of the big coral-pink buttons opening on branches around the corner next the front door. Under a tall hickory along the northern boundary, a carlesii bush has spread to 12 feet. It too blooms freely, but a week or so after the plants espaliered on the south wall. In May the 8-foot fragrant snowball, *V. carlcephalum,* offers a fine carrying scent and larger flowers than most viburnums, but fewer are produced on my plant, which is sunless along the northern boundary.

Late in May the 8-foot doublefile viburnum, *V. plicatum tomentosum,* opens flat white flowers on flat-spreading branches. Give it plenty of room—8 feet or more across, too—and place it as a contrast to upright growers. In fall the brilliant red fruits and bronzy foliage are spectacular.

Also in May the 20-foot *V. sieboldii* opens large, rounded, white clusters followed by red late-summer fruits that turn black. Here it flourishes in fairly deep shade with only a little sky shine to encourage the top. This viburnum can be trained to tree form, and is best so handled in a small garden, for it grows fast.

For June, there are two viburnums at least. Dockmackie, *V. acerifolium,* is low-growing, only 4 to 5 feet. It tolerates heavier shade than the others but, of course, is more floriferous in half-shade. The fragrant white flowers turn into red then black fruits, a delight

My favorite deciduous shrub, the fragrant pink snowball *Viburnum carlesii,* espaliered here on a south wall, blooms profusely from late April to early May before the Christmas-berry-tree casts heavy summer shade. GEORGE TALOUMIS PHOTO

to the birds that may strip this and the other viburnums of berries almost before they are formed.

Also for June is the 10-foot tea viburnum, *V. setigerum,* with small fragrant flowers becoming bright-red fruits. Bloom is sparse on my giant shrub crowded into a north corner with tall andromedas. I have seen it put on a handsome performance in more generous quarters in half-shade.

Shrubs

FLOWERING AND FRUITING SHRUBS FOR LIGHT AND DEEP SHADE

If you plant for a seasonal sequence, these offer marvelous decorative possibilities from early March to frost. Many bloom more fully in the sun but are still satisfactory performers in shade. If you have shade with poor drainage, consult the last section under Miscellany.

Name	Height in Feet	Description	Culture	Remarks
Abelia grandiflora Glossy Abelia	3–4 and as wide	Pink-white tubular flowers, June–Oct.	Half-shade only; needs protected location, not always weather proof, hardy to southern Connecticut.	Not the greatest but useful for long-blooming and semi-evergreen habit. Dwarf 'Edward Goucher' deeper pink.
Abeliophyllum distichum White-forsythia	5 and mounding	Mid-April flowers with a honey scent before leaves.	Light to deep shade, or sun, good for a sun-to-shade situation; tolerates alkalinity.	Good for early bloom; hardy though flower buds not always weatherproof except in a protected location.

Aronia arbutifolia Red Chokeberry	5–6	Native; small white spring flowers, abundant red berries and rich red autumn foliage, irregular form, native.	For moist soil, light to deep shade.	Black chokeberry, *A. melanocarpa*, to 3′; more shapely but less shade tolerant.
Azalea, see *Rhododendron*				
Bayberry, see *Myrica*				
Berberis thunbergii Japanese Barberry	4–5	Small white spring flowers, red berries through most of winter, good autumn foliage color.	Endures deep shade and dry soil, a prickly barrier or bank plant.	Dependable even in worst situations. 'Minor' 12 to 18″, dense growth, good for low hedge. 'Crimson Pigmy', 8–10″, if you want a *red* hedge.
Bridalwreath, see *Spiraea*				
Buttercup-shrub, see *Potentilla*				

Name	Height in Feet	Description	Culture	Remarks
Calycanthus floridus Strawberry-shrub	5	April–June brown-purple fragrant flowers, leaves and bark, all aromatic, native. 'Mrs. Henry' good choice.	Half-shade or sun, undemanding, endures a poorly drained place.	Cut pieces to force indoors to scent winter rooms or bureau drawers; hardly ornamental but delights children.
Chaenomeles (Cydonia) speciosa (japonica) Flowering Quince	1½–6	May, before shiny leaves; white, pink, red, orange flowers.	I have seen heavy bloom under locusts; enjoys some lime.	Makes a strong prickly hedge, low specimens nice to work into foundation areas. Lovely hybrids: pink 'Cameo', red 'Knap Hill', white 'Nivalis'.
Clethra alnifolia Summersweet, Sweet Pepperbush	6–9	Fragrant white spikes of bloom, July–Aug., fine carrying scent, native.	For moist soil and high shade; will endure wet, poorly drained site.	Also a pink form, 5–6', white preferable in a woodland setting, as here under tall trees; accepts sheltered seashore conditions.

Cotoneaster dielsiana	5–6	Pink flowers on arching branches in spring; scarlet berries and foliage in autumn.	One of the few cotoneasters for shade.	Bearberry cotoneaster, *C. dammeri*, semievergreen to 1′; good groundcover for shade.
Daphne mezereum February Daphne	3	Far-reaching fragrance; late Mar., rarely Feb. here.	High shade, sometimes naturalizes.	Choice and revels in cold. Magenta or white flowers; scarlet berries in June.
Deutzia gracilis	2–3	May, bell-like white flowers in panicles.	Blooms even in quite heavy shade, also in sun.	Good for front of a border planting or anywhere a free-flowering smaller shrub is desirable.
Flowering Quince, see *Chaenomeles*				
Forsythia spectabilis and varieties Goldenbells	10	Late Apr.–May flowers before leaves; mostly deep yellow; 'Spring Glory' paler; also dwarf and weeping forms.	Arching growth in light shade or sun. Pruning to keep fountain form makes it more attractive.	Fast-growing, endures city conditions, handsome as specimen or for tall boundary planting; here flourishes under a greedy poplar.

Name	Height in Feet	Description	Culture	Remarks
Fothergilla gardenii	3	Honey-scented white little bottlebrush blooms, late Apr. before leaves, native.	Prefers moist soil, best in part-shade.	From southern Appalachians but adaptable here in protected places; gorgeous fall color well displayed in front of evergreens. *F. monticola* to 6' has spreading growth, bigger blooms.
Franklinia alatamaha	5	White flowers, Aug. to frost with a tea scent, native.	Open shade or sun, here in fairly deep shade, rich acid soil.	Tree to 30' in South; my shrub to 5'. I prize the late waterlily blooms. (Autumn color only in sun.)
Gaylussacia frondosa Wild Huckleberry	6	Tiny, bell-shaped greenish flowers; edible fruits, native.	Shade, acid soil. I enjoy it along the driveway where the poplar shade is heavy.	Fine fall coloring; mine "collected" from a friend's property.

Hamamelis vernalis Vernal Witch-hazel	9	Small yellow ribbon flowers, yeasty scent, sometimes opens as early as late Feb. Golden fall coloring; native.	Flourishes in partial shade.	Be sure to cut some Jan. pieces to open indoors in a sunny window. Harbinger of flowering season.
Hibiscus syriacus Shrub-althea Rose-of-Sharon	5	Summer-to-fall flowers, white, pink, purple, variegated.	Light shade or sun; trouble-free; tolerates poor drainage.	Many cultivars, not a distinguished plant, singles best; endures city and seashore conditions. Useful for midseason color.
Hydrangea arborescens 'Grandiflora'	3–5	Rounded white heads late June–July bloom, 4–7" across, native.	Prune hard in Apr.; heavy flowers on a few branches may break them.	Called Hills of Snow, an old favorite, cool summer effect if you like hydrangeas.
quercifolia Oakleaf Hybrid (See also Climbing Hydrangea in Vine Chart.)	4–6	Erect conical panicles in mid-July, native.	May die to ground in winter, will make a good bush again but with fewer flowers.	Fine red fall color. *H. macrophylla*, the pink and blue seashore favorites need sun.

Name	Height in Feet	Description	Culture	Remarks
Hypericum calycinum St. Johnswort	1–1½	Bright-yellow flowers late July through summer, almost evergreen where hardy.	Endures dry, sandy soil, good groundcover.	May not winter well north of New York City.
Japanese Barberry, see *Berberis*				
Kerria japonica	4–5 as wide	Bright-yellow May bloom, light through summer, heavy in fall.	Good bloom in deep shade; heat-and-drought resistant, likes lime.	Bright-green twigs a winter asset. 'Pleniflora' is double and more likely to need sun, sometimes called globeflower.
Lilac, see *Syringa*				
Lonicera fragrantissima Winter Honeysuckle	6	Tiny piercingly sweet fragrant flowers before leaves, late Feb.–Apr.	Half-shade here under an arbor, but open to winter and early spring sun.	Choice, leaves hold well into Jan.; can be pruned to arching form. One of my indispensables for its far-reaching scent. (Hard to locate in nurseries.)

Mock-orange,
see *Philadelphus*

Name	Size	Description	Culture	Remarks
Myrica pensylvanica Bayberry	6 as wide	Aromatic foliage, gray berries, native.	For light or deep shade; tolerates poor soil or flourishes in good soil.	You could make candles from the berries; nice in deep shade here at outer reaches of place.
Paeonia suffruticosa (Moutan) Tree Peony	3–4 as wide	Pink, red, white, yellow (*lutea*), single and double blooms, mid-May before herbaceous type.	Half-shade, rich soil; take care not to cut off *permanent* woody frame.	Blooms well under my thorn tree at the edge of the terrace; gets a few hours *late* afternoon sun.
Philadelphus coronarius Mock-orange	9	Late May–June, white scented flowers, old-fashioned familiar plant.	Species tolerant quite deep shade here; also 'Belle Etoile'.	Prune all of them after blooming to keep stocky, not thin at base.
cultivars	3–6	Singles and doubles, June–July; 3' 'Silver Showers' nice dwarf; 'Innocence' to 6'.		Select in-bloom plants to check fragrance. Use big growers where plenty of space.

Name	Height in Feet	Description	Culture	Remarks
Potentilla fruticosa Bush Cinquefoil Buttercup-shrub	3	Golden June–Oct. flowers, fine-cut leaves, native. 'Katherine Dykes' pleasing pale yellow, 2½'.	Very hardy, partial shade or sun.	Good in front of border or with evergreen background beside house; useful for long bloom, outstanding, makes a nice low hedge.
Red Chokeberry, see *Aronia*				
Rhododendron—Azalea Species and Hybrids (See also pages 169ff.)	3–12	April–June, white, pink, rose, yellow, scarlet; many fragrant, some evergreen, most species native. (See this chapter for names.)	Acid humusy soil; moisture, mulch, wind protection, for light shade or shifting sunlight; rarely blooms in deep shade.	Species lovely here in open woodland, some very tall; hybrids good specimens or in groups; as here with white birch and hemlocks. Indispensable. (See also chart of Evergreen Shrubs.)
Rose-of-Sharon, see *Hibiscus*				
Shrub-althea, see *Hibiscus*				

Snowberry, see *Symphoricarpos*				
Spiraea prunifolia Bridalwreath	9	Small white button blooms, mid-May.	Shade or sun, no problem.	Red-orange autumn color, pleasing, not spectacular.
x *vanhouttei*	5	Flat white clusters, late May.		Arching growth, showy glaucus foliage, makes a handsome informal hedge.
St. Johnswort, see *Hypericum*				
Strawberry-shrub, see *Calycanthus*				
Summersweet, see *Clethra*				
Sweet Pepperbush, see *Clethra*				
Symphoricarpos albus laevigatus Snowberry	4–5	Clusters of very small pink flowers, mid-June, large white fruits in autumn, native.	Excellent for dense shade.	Good fruiting shrub for birds, not exactly my favorite.

Name	Height in Feet	Description	Culture	Remarks
Syringa Lilac	3–9	Pink *S. microphylla* 'Superba', fall repeater; purple 'Ludwig Spaeth' covered with flowers here in sky shine with no sun.	Best to try for light shade; wood ashes and 5–10–5 fertilizer in spring.	If you love lilacs, try them in full light even without sun—maybe yes, maybe no!
Tree Peony, see *Paeonia*				
Vernal Witch-hazel, see *Hamamelis*				
Viburnum acerifolium Dockmackie, Maple-leaved Viburnum	4–5	Early-June white flowers, red to black fruit, fine autumn foliage, native.	Endures heavier shade than other viburnums; light flowering here.	Indispensable clan. All viburnums floriferous in light shade. Birds like viburnum fruits; I like the fragrant flowers.
x *carlcephalum* Fragrant Snowball	8	White flowers in May, fine carrying scent.	Half-shade, average soil (acid here), undemanding once established.	Large blooms, fine plant; will endure a damp, poorly drained condition.

carlesii Pink Snowball	8 as wide	Late Apr.–May coral blooms, very fragrant.	Under Christmas-berry-tree where spring sun strikes, blooms pale and earlier than in north location under late-leafing hickory; heavy bloom both locations.	Blooms only for 10 days but absolutely essential; nice to train vinelike as here beside plant window; it looks in.
plicatum tomentosum Doublefile Viburnum	9 as wide	Late May, flat white flowers on flat branches; brilliant red fruits in Aug.	Good bloom here in fairly heavy shade.	Horizontal growth, effective contrast to pyramidal growers; needs a lot of room.
setigerum (*theiferum*) Tea Viburnum	10	June, small fragrant flowers then red fruits.	Here in deep north shade sparse flowering deserves a more open location.	Bronze fall foliage, a fine tall shrub, seldom seen.
sieboldii Siebold Viburnum	20	May, large rounded white clusters; red fruits turning black; handsome leaves.	Flourishes here in fairly deep shade with only a little sky shine.	Handsome as a specimen, can be trained to tree form; one of the best viburnums but not for small gardens, needs a lot of room.

Name	Height in Feet	Description	Culture	Remarks
Viburnum continued *trilobum* American Cranberry-bush	12	Marvelous red fruits, start coloring late July, hang into winter, native.		Big and beautiful.
White-forsythia, see *Abeliophyllum*				
Winter Honeysuckle, see *Lonicera*				

BROADLEAF AND NEEDLE SHRUBS FOR SHADE

Most of these plants require shade; they do not merely tolerate it. Light shade suits them all; if deep shade is endured, it is indicated. Here many flourish and bloom under high-pruned oaks in my woodland garden, and even under maples on the brook bank.

Name	Height in Feet	Description	Remarks
Andromeda, see *Pieris*			
Azalea, see *Rhododendron*			
Bamboo, see *Nandina*			
Barberry, see *Berberis*			
Bayberry, see *Myrica*			
Berberis candidula Paleleaf Barberry	2	Little yellow flowers in May, purplish fruits.	These species with leathery foliage are all fairly low-growing or can be kept so by shearing; fruiting not so heavy in shade as in sun. Hardy to zero.
x *chenaultii* Chenault Barberry	4	Inconspicuous white-to-yellow flowers in May; blue-black fall fruits; shiny green leaves.	

Name	Height in Feet	Description	Remarks
Berberis continued			
triacanthophora Three-spine Barbery	4	Thorny, good barrier unclipped.	
verruculosa Warty Barberry	4	One of the best of the evergreen barberries, late bloomer (June), bronze fall foliage.	
Box, see *Buxus*			
Buxus microphylla Littleleaf Box	2–3	From Japan, fine foliage, one of the hardiest.	Shade or sun. Excellent for a low hedge, sheared or natural, but leaves may brown in exposed places. See newer cultivars, 'Compacta', 'Tide Hill', and 'Wintergreen'.
sempervirens Common Box	20	Native to southern Europe; much planted in Colonial gardens; sometimes called American box.	Marvelous shining hedge or accent plant, slow-growing, may be sheared or not. 'Inglis' (hardy to 20° F.) and 'Welleri' good cultivars.
suffruticosa True Dwarf Box	3	Not for very cold or windy areas or dry summers.	Fine for edging, can be kept low.

Cotoneaster apiculata Cranberry Cotoneaster	2	Semievergreen; crimson fruits on long, arching branches.	Larger fruits and a better plant than the familiar rockspray, *C. horizontalis*, which is a scrawiy thing.
salicifolia floccosa	15	Semievergreen to evergreen; small arching plant, red berries in fall, good autumn color.	Particularly good in mid-South, rather like *C. horizontalis* but fruit larger.
Daphne cneorum Garland or Rose Daphne	½	Very fragrant, pink flowers mid-May, sometimes to Dec.	Difficult but worth effort; may die unexpectedly. Needs winter protection, cool moist roots, loose sweet soil.
Enkianthus campanulatus Redvein Enkianthus	10–12	Yellow bellflowers veined red in May; glorious fall coloring.	Somewhat moist, acid soil, same as for rhododendrons; unusual broadleaf to associate with pieris, leucothoe, laurel, etc.
Euonymus fortunei 'Sarcoxie' Columnar Euonymus	5–6	Attractive columnar growth.	Good for beside steps where there is too little room for a spreading plant like a yew.

Name	Height in Feet	Description	Remarks
Euonymus continued *patens* Spreading Euonymus	6	Compact, a really hardy carefree plant, resembles *E. fortunei vegetus* climber.	Good for a very shaded corner or north location under trees.
Hemlock, see *Tsuga*			
Ilex crenata Japanese Holly	5–10	Beautiful small-leaved mounded growth. 'Helleri' and 'Stokes', fine forms.	Species excellent, fast-growing, undemanding, nice for doorways or with small flowering trees as here along driveway; can be pruned to 5 feet; cultivars, as 'Convexa' and 'Rotundifolia' dwarf and compact to 4 feet. Light shade, requires moisture.
glabra Inkberry	6–8	Graceful form; interesting black berries, native.	A white-berried form 'Ivory Queen'.
opaca American Holly	40	Handsome tree; female with brilliant crop of red berries, native.	Plant a male tree (can be small) nearby to insure fruiting of female; needs leaf-miner protection; can be shrub or tree.

Kalmia latifolia Mountain-laurel	5–10	June, pink-white shell-like flowers, also deeper pink-to-red clones, native.	Easy to keep low by pruning; one of the very best. Blooms better in sun but a fine plant in shade with or without flowers. If it ever winterkills, cut to the ground; it will renew.
Leucothoe catesbaei Drooping Leucothoe	3	May–June, waxy-white fragrant pendent flowers, native.	Stands heavy shade here. Small graceful shrub, good in association here with andromeda and mountain-laurel nice bronze fall and winter color.
Ligustrum amurense Amur Privet	10–12	Glossy semievergreen; small white summer flowers; blue-black berries.	All privets stand city conditions well. Light not deep shade; good hedge plants for clipping; hardy.
obtusifolium regelianum Regel Privet	4–5	Most graceful privet; best deciduous privet; horizontal branching; June bloom, blue-black berries.	Clip or not, handsome plant unclipped if you have space.
vulgare Common Privet	10–15	Semievergreen; white summer flowers, shiny black berries.	Flowers have a heavy, musty scent, not always pleasant close by.

Name	Height in Feet	Description	Remarks
Mahonia aquifolium Oregon Holly-grape	3–5	May, fragrant chartreuse flowers; prickly stalks. Prune to keep fairly low and bushy; blue summer berries, native.	Can be rampant, traveling far by underground runners, but usually controlled in shade. Lovely here with laurel and ferns against west housewall for protection; bronze fall color.
bealei Leatherleaf Mahonia	4–6	Pale-yellow fragrant flowers, black fruit.	No autumn color change, less hardy in Northeast.
Mountain-laurel, see *Kalmia*			
Myrica pensylvanica Bayberry	6 as wide	Aromatic foliage, gray berries, native. Semi-evergreen, a rangy grower.	For light or deep shade; tolerates poor soil or flourishes in good soil. You could make candles from berries; nice in deep shade here at outer reaches of place.
Nandina domestica Heavenly Bamboo	5–6	Small white flowers, June–July; dark-red berries in fall; semievergreen.	Humusy soil, light shade, protected place in North; handsome fall foliage.
Oregon Holly-grape, see *Mahonia*			

Pieris floribunda Mountain Andromeda	6	Upright, white pyramidal clusters, May, native.	Semishade; hardy native, fine for on-view plantings out of the sun; here it blooms beside steps to the brook and under the fairly deep shade of a sugar maple.
japonica Japanese Andromeda	9	In mid-April, nodding fragrant clusters of open flowers; young leaves a pleasing bronze in spring.	This thrives in a northern house angle, flower "braids" interesting all winter. 'Pygmaea' to 3' for smaller quarters.
Privet, see *Ligustrum*			
Prunus laurocerasus schipkaensis Schipka Cherry-laurel	9	White racemes late in May; horizontal growth, shiny rich green foliage.	Hardier than species; shines out in a shaded planting, rapid grower.
Rhododendron—Azalea Gable, Glenn Dale, Exbury, Knap Hill, Kurume Hybrids	5–10	May–June, pink, white, yellow, orange, red.	High shade of oaks or open pines; acid humusy soil; protect from wind; supply mulch. These may prove evergreen; it depends on location and weather. For color select in-bloom plants in a nursery. Among very best bloomers for shade.

Name	Height in Feet	Description	Remarks
Rhododendron catawbiense Catawba Rhododendron	8	Mid-June, white, pink, red; big spreading plant, native.	Native, good for northern locations; allow 6′ for most.
carolinianum Carolina Rhododendron	5–6	White to purple, native.	Some hybrids of this will stand, even prefer, considerable shade, as 'Windbeam'.
maximum Rosebay	12	Pink to white, June–July, native.	This one makes a 12′ spread.
Schipka Cherry-laurel, see *Prunus*			
Skimmia japonica Japanese Skimmia	2	White spring blooms, then red fruit.	Part shade, both male and female plants necessary for bloom; needs protected location to survive this far north. Mine has pulled through nicely sheltered by laurel bushes and a wall.
Taxus baccata 'Repandens' English Yew	4	Nearly prostrate; leaves blue-green; flat-topped with pendulous branch tips.	All yews thrive in shade, even on north side of house here; most accommodating, hardiest of English yews for us.

cuspidata 'Densa' Dwarf Japanese Yew	4 to 5	Spreading.	Judicious pruning keeps it low; no shearing necessary; can spread to 20′ across.
x *media* 'Hatfieldii' Hatfield Yew	10	Broadly columnar.	For corners of house, not beside front door. Both this and 'Hicksii' can be trimmed for narrow hedge.
'Hicksii' Hicks Yew	6	Narrow columnar.	Excellent for hedge or accent.
Tsuga canadensis Hemlock	to 60	Very beautiful needle evergreen; graceful drooping branches, shapely; fast-spreading growth, native.	Many flourish here under patches of open sky and grow in quite deep shade of some giant deciduous trees. Indispensable.

Yew, see *Taxus*

Pendent yellow clusters, resembling wisteria, open late in May on this shapely laburnum tree at the northeast corner of this house.
GEORGE TALOUMIS PHOTO

10

SMALLER TREES
FOR YOUR SHADED PLACE

Accent on Bloom

It is not easy to restrain my enthusiasm when I write about the smaller trees, those that rarely go beyond 30 feet. These can be pruned high to serve as shade trees on the lawn or to bring loveliness to a property *under* the big shade trees that are also pruned high. You won't get the gorgeous effulgence in shade that many flowering trees produce in sun but you will enjoy respectable bloom just as I have. Here the big shade trees have gradually encroached upon them so that they are mostly denied even half sunlight but, still, all those I have suggested do well in light shade. Of course, mine are regularly fertilized in spring and never suffer drought in summer.

But before we talk about the flowering trees, I must call your attention to two of my favorite smaller trees without flowers—the gray birch and the Japanese maple. I love the gray birch—only it's really white and a pretty multiple-trunk tree. I have planted it everywhere I could as accent. Mostly it has prospered but not the clumps I set out in fairly deep shade behind a laburnum. Those declined steadily. Since this tree is indispensable to me, I have learned to give it more agreeable locations, as opposite the kitchen window where it gets a couple of hours of morning sun and then full light, as accent and terminal point to the Fern Garden where the trees are open to the sky, and with azaleas beside the Round Garden. There the azaleas get what sun there is and the white birch clump associating with the dark-green hemlock and a tall box-elder still gets full light. Wherever you plant birches, their gold-coin autumn color will delight you. If you have space for some smaller trees and are not put off by yearly spraying for birch miner (or attention to a systemic, which is easy enough to insert in the soil), you may want at least one clump of birch. Impatiens flowers beautifully beneath mine, also Christmas-roses.

Then there is the Japanese maple, but not for me the dark-red maple of hallowed memory too often planted with a blue spruce in Victorian front yards. It's the shaded green or amber-foliage type I admire, like the handsome specimen in our church garden. This one is some 15 feet tall and almost as wide, so consider the eventual spread if you select it. A shapely tree, slow-growing enough to be handled as a shrub if you prefer, it is effective by itself in light shade or in a place open to the sky. Some of the Japanese maples have finely cut leaves, others not so deeply lobed have leaves like stars. They need good soil and a fair amount of moisture. Do select your tree personally for these maples vary greatly in leaf shape and color; also be aware that red spring foliage may turn green in summer. Anyway, don't overlook this one.

For Winter into Spring

The vernal witch-hazel, really more shrub than tree, is for you if you incline to winter weariness toward the end of February and early March. Its fragrant yellow ribbons offer the first color

A choice small tree, the Japanese maple, shades a raised bed of liriope, hosta, and epimedium, impatiens at the corner, the whole contained by railroad ties, strong support for plantings above the surrounding grade. Design by Jack Valle Inc. CHARLES MARDEN FITCH PHOTO

here, expanding on warm days, wisely closing tight when the temperature drops. I enjoy it not only in the shade of the big maple at the back of the Round Garden but also indoors. Branches cut in January soon open in a sunny window bringing a pleasant yeasty scent to the living room.

The Cornelian-cherry—only it's a dogwood—offers an abundance of small yellow fluffs in March before the big trees leaf out. The fluffs are really flowers, much the same that we see as *centers* when the familiar dogwood encircles them with white bracts in May. Here, next to tall lilacs, the Cornelian-cherry, naturally spreading, is pruned high and thin and valued for its early bloom with the first bulbs.

Almost as cold-defying, the spicebush, native to our eastern woodlands, early in April opens tiny yellow fragrant flowers before the foliage. You can grow this as a shrub or tree, for it rarely goes

On the north side of a house, a four-pronged gray birch is a handsome sight seen from the house; below it thrive evergreens in a bed of pachysandra. GEORGE TALOUMIS PHOTO

above 15 feet; and, if you have a wild garden, it will please you there. Quite deep shade does not deter the spicy blooms, but soil moisture is essential. The foliage turns clear gold in fall and, when it is gone, you see a wealth of red berries if your plant is pistillate (female).

The April–May Peak

Now is the brightest season of tree bloom. The shadbush, likely to be the tallest, even to 40 feet, opens upright clusters of single white flowers in April. It is a shapely grower and, if you have a very small garden, perhaps a patterned type, this would look nice in the center. Early in summer there is a wealth of red berries, all too soon stripped by the birds. This native has other fine qualities, brilliant red-to-yellow fall foliage and conspicuous gray bark in winter.

Just a little later, and sometimes with the shadblow, a beautiful pair, both natives, begin to bloom in unison, the familiar white dogwood and the purple-pink redbud. To be avoided is this redbud next a dark-red Japanese maple, or a pink dogwood, really eye-searing combinations. The redbud, whose dried seedpods are hardly ornamental, has the advantage of brilliant fall foliage, a glowing yellow, nice contrast to the dogwood crimson. Both redbud and dogwood bloom before leaves unfold.

To me the white dogwood is prettier than the pink, particularly with other woodland plants. According to a story, all the pinks are descended from a single branch that sported pink on a white tree in a Wissahickon nursery near Philadelphia some years ago. However, records in Williamsburg, Virginia, indicate that the pink dogwood was known there in 1737. At Stony Brook Cottage there are a number of whites blooming well in more or less shade, deeper under the tall poplar beside the driveway, lighter fairly close to the sweetgum near the house, and again considerable in the Round Garden where a white dogwood gives shade to ferns and hostas, itself accepting the shadow of the wild cherry.

You can make your dogwood a lawn tree by pruning the horizontal growth high or you can let branches almost sweep the ground as I have with one tree. The dogwood is ever beautiful, not just in bloom. From late summer to fall, as the birds permit, it is covered with clusters of shiny red berries; autumn foliage is a fine crimson, and then there are the decorative gray buds of winter. Shade or half-shade, which means a little shifting sunshine or good light, as in an open place, suits this admirable *Cornus florida,* and I am particular about deep watering in summer. You can select forms like the narrow upright 'Fastigiata' or the graceful drooping 'Pendula', various pink shades, increasing bract numbers nearing doubleness, or foliage variegation, but horizontal planes and pure white blooms of the type-species suit me to a T.

To extend the dogwood season, there is *Cornus kousa.* I was so pleased when I discovered this *less-known* species. It blooms in June, some three weeks after *C. florida,* is not so tall and is admittedly less distinguished. It can also be grown as a bushy shrub and tolerates considerable shade here. It has the same bright berry-like fruits, and the crimson foliage holds until mid-November.

But to return to our April-into-May sequence, the native silverbells are well worth your regard. In *more* than half-shade here, and pruned to umbrella form, the Carolina silverbell, *Halesia carolina,* strings white bells along the underside of its leafless branches late April into May; in due course, the foliage gives heavy shade to perennials in the bed below. The seedpods are interesting—or a nuisance, according to your point of view—and this tree like the great or mountain silverbell, *Halesia monticola,* prefers acid soil. Blooming about the same time in the meadow, the larger trees grow to 40 feet in time, offer larger flowers and golden autumn foliage. I rarely see the silverbells in other gardens, but if you have room for a number of flowering trees, you will certainly enjoy one. The smaller *Halesia carolina* can easily be made part of your garden; pruned high, it makes a good small shade tree on the lawn. The new form *H. vestita verticillata* is offered as a rounded tree with larger and more abundant flowers, the clear white tinged with rose-pink—sounds nice. (See Color Section.)

The saucer magnolia *M. x soulangiana,* makes a brave beginning at 2 to 3 feet when enormous white-to-purple flowers (white inside, color outside) start to open before the leaves late April to May. This spectacular tree needs plenty of room, to some 15 feet, for it grows almost as broad as high. I loved it in my Philadelphia garden, where its exotic appearance seemed appropriate, and there it flourished in considerable shade. It should be transplanted in spring while small and assured rich soil and adequate moisture. The native sweet bay, *M. virginiana,* blooms later, its fragrant waxy white flowers opening June into July. Here it is deciduous, evergreen in the South.

Then before summer, there is the May-tree, the English hawthorn that turns the whole of England into a garden in spring.

The dogwood, growing naturally at the edge of woodland, is one of the showiest of all the smaller flowering trees. Here in full light, a handsome white-flowering specimen blooms freely in association with shade-tolerant evergreens—rhododendrons, mountain-laurel. yews, and junipers. GEORGE TALOUMIS PHOTO

Growing quickly to some 15 feet, mine at the west side of the terrace and considerably shaded by maples, has spread as wide, well over the terrace roof. It is pruned to keep from touching, and I enjoy the branches spreading there under my bedroom casements. Flat white blooms cover the tree in May, scarlet fruits in autumn cling into winter. Let alone, the branches would sweep the ground but I had my tree pruned up to 8 feet to allow a spread of evergreen myrtle and early daffodils in the shady part below, and tree peonies on the south reaching out to the sun.

And while we are on hawthorns, I want to mention two for June. I like the native cockspur thorn blooming a little later than the English hawthorn and prized particularly for the clusters of little red-apple fruits that cling into winter and the handsome orange-to-scarlet fall foliage. This thorn tree is taller, to 25 feet.

The Washington thorn, *C. phaenopyrum,* a native of about the same height, blooms in mid-June but with such heavy fall fruiting that it gives the impression of a second flowering, this time red not white. (A word of warning, don't plant hawthorns near junipers because they are the alternate host for cedar-apple rust. Anyway, junipers need full sun and the hawthorns tolerate shade so the combination is unlikely on the home place.)

Before we move into the delirium of June, there is a yellow-flowering tree for mid-May that is a pleasing change from the whites and pinks of the earlier season. My laburnum is planted near sassafras and box-elder that are always trying to press in upon it and so has only a smidgin of sunshine there at the outer edge of the deep southern boundary planting. Grateful for its early summer beauty, I always remember to water it deeply, almost every other week if we get no heavy rain from June to September.

June

As spring moves into summer, it is the annuals and perennials rather than the flowering trees that bring color to the shaded place. However, three trees are to be considered, and for me one is indispensable. I cannot recommend too heartily to you the fringetree which has given me years of pleasure. Partly shaded here by the sweetgum with just a few hours of somewhat distant southern sunshine, the fringetree is an experience. In June, the white silken panicles, like embroidery floss, fill the whole house with a delectable sweet-clover scent when I leave the front door open. This pleasure lasts for only two weeks. Then the bloom gives way to foliage—this is about the last tree to leaf out—and I have to sweep and sweep for there is a great clutter of fading flowers. If this is likely to bother you, don't plant your tree next to a door or terrace. Since the fragrance of the staminate (male) trees is far-reaching, you can even enjoy it planted at a little distance. I like multiple trunks on the fringetree and prune tops to arch over steps and walks, and the gray trunks are pleasing in winter. Here above the deep roots grows a whole garden of lilies, bulbs, and myrtle.

About the same time the mountain-ash, a fine lawn tree that may grow to 35 feet, but not quickly, opens white flowers in June followed by spectacular clusters of orange-red fruit late in summer, and this hangs on into early winter. You can select a hybrid, 'White Wax' or 'Carpet of Gold', instead of this species. If you'd prefer white or yellow fruit, the yellow-to-red autumn foliage is another asset of this nice symmetrical tree.

Carrying white bloom—the bells hang from every twig—and fragrance into July, the Japanese snowbell makes a pleasing vase-shaped tree for lawn or border background. It is not exacting as to soil or site and even endures city conditions with grace. Too little grown and too seldom offered, you may not find this at your local nursery but mail-order houses may be able to supply you even if they don't list it because of their small stock. Just write to inquire; that's how I locate rare and wonderful plants I want.

Crab Apples

Again, I feel I must say how variable is the measurement of shade, and perhaps it makes a difference whether shade has gradually come upon the flowering trees after they are established, as here, or if they are first planted in shade. In any case, I can only relay to you my own experience and observation. You may find the shade *you* have permits a wider—or unhappily—a narrower range of material. I am a little hesitant to make this suggestion, yet I must speak about the handsome crab apples, generally advised for full sun, and I have one pair in such a location. Then at the side of the driveway with the neighbor's big maple towering above it, and only about two hours of early eastern sunshine, I have a Japanese crab apple, *Malus floribunda,* now about 25 feet tall. It blooms pink and double early in May, and is covered with yellow and red fruits from late August to mid-October. Growth and bloom are heavy so that pruning to keep it open and shapely is necessary at least every other year.

Then a Sargent crab, so lovely in bloom, flourishes partway up the hill in fairly deep shade. This one, usually more shrub than tree, has been kept to one trunk with branches coming out of it about a foot up. It is a mighty spreader—now 10 feet across— and is occupying its present location because, planted as a delightful *little* thing, it soon outgrew the driveway bed and had to be moved. The small white flowers, like a lace mantle, open mid-May and are followed by red fruits. If you are very fond of crab apples but have a quite shady place, you might try these two in as open a location as possible, but there is no guarantee given with this suggestion.

Finally

Our flowering season began with the yellow vernal witch-hazel in bloom late in February in the Round Garden. Now it ends with another native witch-hazel opening sweet-scented spidery yellow flowers across the brook late in October. Witch-hazels may not be the most important flowering trees but they brighten lightly shaded places for those who have room for a late-winter to late-fall pageant.

Finally suppose you admire this long succession but have space for only a few trees. What to choose? Hard-pressed, I'd probably say dogwood for late April–May, fringetree for June, Japanese snowbell for June–July. Or, you could have a spring splurge— shadbush, redbud, and silverbell. But don't depend on me; see the trees yourself, and maybe you can have more than three.

SMALLER TREES—MOSTLY FLOWERING—FOR YOUR SHADED PLACE

These bloom under high-pruned trees, in fully light locations, or in half-shade, half-sun. Plant with plenty of space between them so that more air can compensate for less sun.

Name	Height in Feet	Flowers, Fruits, Foliage	Remarks
Acer palmatum Japanese Maple	20	Shapely tree for foliage shaded green (my favorite), or red-purple, or yellow to pink to orange; some with finely cut leaves. Needs good soil and moisture.	Handsome specimens for light shade; slow growing; select in nursery to get the foliage type and color you want. The old, overplanted red not the only one.
Amelanchier canadensis Shadbush or Service-berry	30	Single, white, Apr.–May flowers in upright clusters before leaves; red berries in early summer soon stripped by birds; fine native for moist soil and light shade.	Yellow-to-red fall foliage is spectacular; also gray bark in winter; in hot spring weeks flowering may be brief; a slender graceful tree.

Name	Height in Feet	Flowers, Fruits, Foliage	Remarks
Betula populifolia Gray Birch (called White)	25	One of my essentials for full light; pure gold in fall. Tolerates poor soil, thrives in good, requires leaf-miner protection, good hemlock companion; native.	Lovely, white-barked accents for gardens and walks, select at nursery, three- or four-pronged clumps.
Cercis canadensis Eastern Red-bud	30	Purple-pink flowers Apr. into May before leaves; brilliant yellow autumn foliage; among best for light shade; transplant while small; native.	Native New England to Florida, same range as white dogwood, the two, good garden companions. Growth flat at top. Don't plant this next to a red Japanese maple; select the white 'Alba' instead.
Chionanthus virginicus Fringetree	25	Here partly shaded by sweetgum, with only a few hours of afternoon sunshine. Silken white panicles in June; last tree to leaf out; marvelously fragrant; attractive with one or multiple trunks; bright yellow in fall; native.	Utterly beautiful, too little planted; lovely close to the house but better not next terrace because of much shedding; here it arches over step and front walk and for a couple of weeks I must sweep and sweep! Worth the trouble. Prune to suit site.

Cornelian-cherry, see *Cornus*

Cornus florida Flowering Dogwood	25–35	Large, flat white or pink (var. rubra) blooms late Apr.–May; shiny red berries late summer to fall; crimson autumn foliage. Perhaps best of small flowering trees; if space for only one, select this; native.	Needs deep watering in drought, tolerates considerable shade. Horizontal growth; let branches sweep ground or prune high for a small shade tree. Handsome in every season. Blooms here under high-pruned poplar; excellent under oaks.
kousa chinensis Japanese Dogwood	20	White June blooms, red, berrylike fruits, crimson fall foliage into mid-Nov.	Bushy growth, blooms 3 weeks after *C. florida*; nice extension of dogwood season, very shade-tolerant.
mas Cornelian-cherry	15	Small, fluffy yellow blooms in Mar. before trees in leaf; red fall fruits.	Treasured for dependable earliness, naturally spreading but here pruned narrow and upright.
Crab Apple, see *Malus*			
Crataegus oxyacantha English Hawthorn or May-tree	15–20	Very shaded location here. Fragrant, flat, snow-white clusters in May; red autumn fruits that hang into winter; shapely rounded form; thorny and fast-growing.	Don't plant near junipers; allow each a 15-foot spread. Naturally a rounded, low-branched tree. Or prune high and open to see through as here for brook view; fast grower. 'Paul's Scarlet' a good choice.

Name	Height in Feet	Flowers, Fruits, Foliage	Remarks
Crataegus continued *phaenopyrum* Washington Thorn	25	Clusters of mid-June cream-white flowers; fine red fruits, scarlet autumn coloring; native.	Heavy fruiting looks like a second blooming and fruit clings into winter. Deep rooting.
crus-galli Cockspur Thorn	25	White May–June bloom; half-shade; glossy foliage, bright-red little apple fruits hang into winter; native.	Handsome fall foliage, orange to scarlet.
Dogwood, see *Cornus*			
Fringetree, see *Chionanthus*			
Goldenchain-tree, see *Laburnum*			
Halesia carolina Silverbell	25	More than half-shade here; white bells strung along branches late Apr. into May ahead of leaves, deep-rooted enough for perennials underneath, native.	Here pruned high to umbrella shape; interesting seeds, prefers acid soil. Pretty sight when robins hop among the white spring bells.
monticola Great Silverbell	40	Golden autumn coloring, nutlike fruits; large flowers; native.	

Hamamelis virginiana Common Witch-hazel	15	Spidery, very sweet-scented yellow flowers in late Oct. after leaves fall; vase-shaped, native.	Grows in lightly shaded woodland; beautiful finale for the growing season; golden yellow fall foliage.
Hawthorn, see *Crataegus*			
Japanese Maple, see *Acer*			
Japanese Snowbell, see *Styrax*			
Laburnum x *watereri* (*vossii*) Goldenchain-tree	25	Yellow flowers in pendent clusters like wisteria, mid- to late May. Seeds poisonous.	Be sure to water this one in drought. Fine for early yellow, rare color among flowering trees. Blooms here in fairly heavy shade.
Lindera benzoin Benzoin or Spicebush	15	Tiny pale-yellow fragrant flowers early in Apr. ahead of leaves; golden fall foliage, red berries on pistillate (female) plants; eastern native. For low moist soil.	Beautiful volunteer here in the damp shady woods beside the bridge; crushed leaves are aromatic.

Name	Height in Feet	Flowers, Fruits, Foliage	Remarks
Magnolia x soulangiana Saucer Magnolia	20	White to purple-pink, Apr.–May flowers; starts to bloom at 2 to 3 feet; no fall coloring.	Best to transplant magnolias in spring, spectacular trees; need plenty of room.
virginiana (glauca) Sweet Bay Magnolia	25	Waxy white flowers, fragrant, June–July; native.	Good for half-shade, more bush than tree in cold areas; evergreen in South.
Malus floribunda Japanese Flowering Crab Apple	25–30	Deep-pink early-May flowers, late-Aug. to mid-Oct. yellow and red fruits. With maple shade above and 2 hours of eastern sun, this bloomed well for me.	Crab apples are recommended with reservation for shade. If you must have them, set in as open a place as possible.
sargentii Sargent Crab Apple	8	Dainty mid-May flowers cover the tree like a snowfall; red fruits.	In considerable shade here, with a 10-foot spread; branches come out of trunk a foot above ground.
May-tree, see *Crataegus*			
Red-bud, see *Cercis*			

Rowan-tree, see *Sorbus*			
Service-berry or Shadbush, see *Amelanchier*			
Silverbell, see *Halesia*			
Sorbus aucuparia Mountain-ash, Rowan-tree	30–40	For half-and-half shade. Clusters of white flowers in June, brilliant orange-red fruit, much of which clings until early winter.	Fine yellow-to-red autumn coloring; a number of interesting new hybrids, growing only 20 to 25 feet.
Styrax japonica Japanese Snowbell	20–30	Lovely, fragrant white bells hang from every twig June–July; much too little planted; transplant while small.	Beautiful symmetrical vase-shaped tree for light shade. Umbrella form when mature; endures difficult city conditions of soil and location, nice background tree for shrub border.
Sweet Bay Magnolia, see *M. virginiana*			
Witch-hazel, see *Hamamelis*			

One of the most satisfactory vines for shade, the climbing hydrangea, *H. anomala petiolaris,* once established, is a mighty vine that blooms well in the shade. Here, climbing by holdfasts, it clings to a chimney and moves toward the second floor. GEORGE TALOUMIS PHOTO

11

VINES FOR
GROUND-TOWARD-SKY
EFFECTS

*Lusty or Delicate
to Suit Your Purpose*

One early June morning as I pondered the south view from the terrace I beheld a puzzling sight—what appeared to be a foamy white waterfall gushing down from tall shrubs at the back of the heavily shaded Round Garden. Quick inspection revealed that the waterfall was a great arching cane flung down by a wild Japanese multiflora rose. I had noticed the bold invader the year before making its upward way through the tall honeysuckle bush and the witch-hazel tree but the area was rather wild there so I hadn't attempted to rout out the shiny-leaved prickly plant. Here then was my thank-you, this 8-foot vining spray flung into space above the garden seat, the foam produced by pyramids of small white flowers of sweet honeylike fragrance.

The lovely sight gave this overneat gardener a thrill and a lesson. It also reminded me of a "vine" I had forgotten. Whether I should suggest this shade-enduring rose for your garden is a question. Also, roses are not vines but tall plants you must tie

in place if you want them to act like vines. Certainly the multiflora
rose is too madly rampant for a small place but grand for distant
viewing if you have acreage where you can enjoy it trained as
vine or preferably rampant as groundcover. It used to be much
advertised as a "living fence" for boundaries that needed to be
"horse high, bull strong, and goat tight." You and I are unlikely to have such requirements; for us this Japanese rose often
seen now in neglected gardens or beside old abandoned farm-
houses simply offers a lovely white June picture to be enjoyed
from a distance where the inevitable, but harmless, summer mildew
does not matter.

More suitable are a number of flowering, evergreen, and deciduous vines to be chosen according to need. They climb in
various ways—the hydrangea and evergreen wintercreeper by root-
lets or "holdfasts," like little suction disks, powerful as you discover when you try to loosen them from an unwanted situation;
the honeysuckles with twining stems; clematis with twisting leaf
stems; wisteria with powerful canes that circle a support. In any
case, give your vines something to climb on and select them according to their power. Some vines are decorative for a small trellis,
others are violent growers that will take over your house and raise
your roof.

Among these last is the wisteria, a poor choice for shade because it must have sun to produce those gorgeous pendent clusters
of bloom. On my arbor it has bloomed less and less with every
more densely shaded year. If you have a great dead tree to be
concealed, plant this Japanese wisteria beside it; encourage its
early years with food and water and before too long it will
reach 25 feet or so, the stems twisting around the trunk and
gorgeous bloom when the wisteria reaches the sun at the top.

For Flowers

My first choice for flowers is the climbing hydrangea, *H. anomala
petiolaris*. This woody vine climbing by holdfasts has a 75-foot

potential, but I train it sidewise and prune it to *available* space under and around a west casement. There is hardly any sunlight there but the vine blooms handsomely with great, flat white clusters late in June. Expect a slow start; energy for the great climb is not apparent for about two years after planting when it really takes off.

Then there are the honeysuckles. Hall's honeysuckle, *Lonicera halliana,* is an invasive pest but with marvelous June fragrance. Wherever it gets hold, it takes all before it; on my hill we have to mow it down, but oh, that sweet scent! The honeysuckle for a trellis by a window is *L. heckrottii,* 'Goldflame', its rondels of bloom covering every twig end from May until frost. This one is night-fragrant, twining by thick shoots but never strangling, and not reaching much above 8 feet. (Watch for aphids that may appear until July, and spray the vine along with your roses; 'Goldflame' is worth some effort.)

For bloom in almost *half-*shade, there is clematis, a choice vine that adorns the arbor posts along the whole east side of the house. Here with shade at the roots but about 3 hours of morning sun for the tops, the purple 'Ramona', white 'Henryi', and lilac-rose 'Mme. Baron Veillard' bloom luxuriantly; the early pink *C. montana rubens* adorns one end where there is less sun. Next door at my daughter's, clematis vines under honeylocust trees get only about the same hours of western sunshine and still bloom luxuriously. The sweet autumn clematis, *C. paniculata,* for August and September, will bloom with less sun than the large-flowered varieties but it still needs *some* as I discovered when I tried it on an arbor deeply shaded by the apple tree. There it just wouldn't produce. Take care not to plant clematis in such predominantly shaded locations for it will disappoint you. Work lime into the soil at planting time, water deeply through dry summer weeks, and fertilize freely early in spring.

The silverlace-vine, *Polygonum aubertii,* is an excellent choice for a big shaded area. The fragrant foamy flowers open in August on a vine that travels quite quickly for 20 to 25 feet on a sturdy support. In an earlier garden, I planted it to cover a whole

The fast-growing
silverlace-vine, *Polygonum
aubertii,* white and fragrant
at the end of summer,
needs a strong support on
which it will travel quickly
to 25 feet or even higher.
GEORGE TALOUMIS PHOTO

pergola, which it did, but at Stony Brook Cottage it finally defeated me, too difficult to prune on the roof and too weedy as to progeny on the ground. But don't you overlook it for a vast, lightly shaded location or as covering for a shed you don't care to see or a long post-and-rail fence that runs from sun to shade.

Other flowering vines for light shade are the perennial pea to 8 feet—white, pink, or magenta but with no scent—and the blue-and-white passion-vine to 15 feet. Interesting bloom on both, but I haven't used them because they die down in winter.

Evergreen Coverage

First, of course, among evergreen climbers is English ivy, *Hedera helix,* clinging by holdfasts to stone, stucco, brick, or rough wood. It is for sheltered locations in semi- to full shade, never where full winter sun strikes, for it will burn there in dry weather without snow cover. English ivy will not grow well much north of New York City, that is, beyond Zone 6, but where it flourishes it makes a fine, glossy green drapery to 80 feet or so. When you prune it, or any other vine against a house, leave some open spaces to show the brick or stucco background; it looks prettier if the curtain isn't too dense.

Baltic ivy, *H. h. baltica,* growing to 50 feet, with smaller, not so glossy leaves, stands more cold and may be a better choice for you.

The wintercreepers, *Euonymus fortunei,* climbing by holdfasts to about 30 feet, are handsome evergreens, for light to fairly deep shade. They cling to walls, cover banks, and clamber up dead trees. *E. f. radicans* has small leaves and no noticeable flowers; *E. f. vegetus,* often called bigleaf wintercreeper, is similar but glossy, with pinkish berries in fall. I let mine ramble over a big stump beside the brook. Next door, the small-leaved wintercreeper travels mightily over the heavily shaded west wall to the top of a stucco house. These evergreen wintercreepers are likely to be your best choice for shaded house walls.

Deciduous Vines

Tolerant deciduous vines of notable power are good selections for vast spaces, not for trim trellises next the house. *Parthenocissus quinquefolia,* sometimes listed as *Ampelopsis,* the native five-leaved Virginia-creeper or woodbine (poison-ivy is three-leaved) makes a dark shiny covering here over the New England stone fences. With a 75-foot potential, it is a good shade vine, climbing by holdfasts, to cling to stone, wood, or brick walls, or ascend a tree. Its brilliant scarlet hues in early autumn are a delight, so too the tiny blue-black fruits dotting the foliage, attractive to many birds.

The three-leaved Boston-ivy, *P. tricuspidata,* growing to 45 feet, also turns from rich dark green to glowing scarlet in fall but the fruits are less visible until the leaves fall. This vine takes time to get going, then travels fast. Both these climbers can make it to the top of a three-story house in a few years. 'Lowii' is a miniature with "palmlike leaves" and of more restrained nature. You can grow this in a limited space where it will make a charming wall tracery or adornment for a stone gatepost or low wall, and 'Lowii' has the same gorgeous autumn tints.

The porcelain-vine, *Ampelopsis brevipedunculata,* to 30 feet, is valued not only for its shade tolerance but for those lovely fall berries in tints of lavender, green, and aqua. It can be used for dense screening on a wire arbor or big trellis to which it will cling by tendrils. This one has leaves rather like those of the grape.

If it's absolute, impenetrable privacy you want and the location is shaded, plant that old favorite, Dutchmans-pipe, *Aristolochia durior,* growing fast to 30 feet. The inconspicuous brown-purple flowers are more interesting than beautiful and there is no fall coloring, but this twining vine with rounded leaves, sometimes a foot across, may be just the plant to conceal a wall or hide you from the neighbors (or the neighbors from you).

For Bright Berries

I did not plant bittersweet, *Celastrus scandens,* it simply appeared, covering a vast area with its rampant twining growth. Without support it grew at the far edge of the property, rising by its own power to 6 feet and requiring an absolute pruning attack to keep it in hand. Flower arrangers love those curling, yellow-orange, berry-strewn branches, but you must be aware of what bittersweet can do. Furthermore, both male and female plants are necessary for fruiting and in shade the fruiting is less. Best to avoid this wild native thing and instead try the Chinese bittersweet, *C. loeseneri,* which is newly offered and self-fruiting, said to be covered with fruit even in half-shade.

Annual Climbers

Only a few can be recommended for shade. Certainly not the lovely morning glories, which are a real disappointment in shade. And annuals of course are more trouble requiring yearly planting but they are charming. You will get a longer all-summer display if you sow seeds indoors in late March rather than outdoors in May after frost is over in your area and when the soil has warmed up a little later.

The Allegheny vine, *Adlumia fungosa,* bears flowers like the bleedingheart. It's a sweet delicate thing, growing to 15 feet, and charming for a small trellis or to let go among shrubs, which it will not smother. Actually a biennial, it does not bloom until the second year, and then you must sow again.

The cup-and-saucer vine, *Cobaea scandens,* sometimes called cathedral bells, makes a pretty tracery on a trellis. Growing fast to 20 feet, it is covered with green-and-purple flowers from summer to frost.

The black-eyed-Susan vine or clockvine, *Thunbergia alata,* is another delight, with arrow-shaped leaves and round orange-yellow-to-white blooms. I've grown it inside as a pot plant, twining it on a wire tripod support, and then set it outside as a summer doorway accent. It's also pretty for a hanging basket or window box in light shade or for a small trellis. It will hardly reach 10 feet and will be a long delight however you use it.

VINES FOR THE SHADOWS

There are rampant and delicate types to cover a house wall or adorn a small trellis; be sure of the potential of each as you select. (E for Evergreen; D for Deciduous; Semi for Semievergreen)

Name	Height in Feet	Type	Description	Remarks
Akebia quinata Fiveleaf Akebia	20–25	Semi	Twiner with small, fragrant purple flowers late Apr.–May, light to fairly deep shade.	Isolate this one; lovely ferny growth for the right place, but it has mighty root runners and needs space.
American Bittersweet, see *Celastrus scandens*				
Ampelopsis brevipedunculata Porcelain-vine	30	D	Climbs by tendrils; deeply lobed leaves; lavender-pink berries turning blue. Small greenish spring flowers; semishade.	Bright-green foliage makes a dense screen; needs sturdy arbor; prune back halfway early in Mar.
Aristolochia durior Dutchmans-pipe	30	D	Twining woody climber, for thick screening, heart-shaped leaves, brownish purple pipe-shaped May bloom.	Fairly rampant, good to cover a long fence if it is strong, or to make an impenetrable screen for the back porch.

Name	Height in Feet	Type	Description	Remarks
Boston-ivy, see *Parthenocissus*				
Celastrus scandens American Bittersweet	20–30	D	Native, woody climber; good twining cover for a rail fence or can make dense hedging, but don't let it smother valuable shrubs or trees. For light or fairly deep shade.	Glorious yellow-orange fruits on female plants, male plant needed nearby for pollination; too rampant for a limited situation.
Clematis, species and varieties	6–30	D	Handsome spring to fall flowers depending on variety—white, pink, lavender, purple—on twining plants of various heights. Lime essential in soil; water in dry spells.	Species *C.* x *jackmanii* (D) and *C. paniculata* (Semi) endure more shade than large-flowering hybrids; these need roots in shade, but about 3–4 hours of sun for tops
Dutchmans-pipe, see *Aristolochia*				
English Ivy, see *Hedera helix*				

Euonymus fortunei radicans	E	30	Among finest evergreen climbers for shade. Small dark leaves on vines that cling by holdfasts to stone walls, cover trees, banks.	Good evergreen coverage; *E. f.* 'Kewensis', miniature type, smallest leaves, also good groundcover in shade.
vegetus Bigleaf Wintercreeper			Larger glossy leaves, orange-red berries.	
Fleece-vine, see *Polygonum*				
Hedera helix English Ivy	E	80	Woody vine, shiny lobed leaves, climbs by holdfasts, good cover for stone, stucco walls.	Fast-growing in moist soil with humus. Avoid winter sun. (See also Groundcovers.)
var. *baltica*	E	50	Small leaves, not so glossy.	Somewhat hardier, less prone to winter injury.
Honeysuckle, see *Lonicera*				
Hydrangea anomala petiolaris Climbing Hydrangea	D	50	Probably best flowering vine for semishade; handsome white June–July flowers; more style than bush types.	Needs rich soil; climbs by holdfasts nailed to a west corner wall here, indispensable. Takes time to develop, then grows madly, needs pruning control.

Name	Height in Feet	Type	Description	Remarks
Lonicera japonica 'Halliana' Hall's Honeysuckle	30	D	Vine with twining stems, very fragrant white-to-yellow July–Aug. bloom; light to deep shade with fewer flowers.	Plant only where rampant weedy growth can be tolerated; will smother trees or shrubs, but scent is divine!
sempervirens Trumpet Honeysuckle	20		May–Aug. scarlet-yellow flowers but no scent; half-shade.	Native twiner; red fruits.
Parthenocissus quinquefolia Virginia-creeper, Woodbine	75	D	Rampant woody vine, 5 leaflets, blue-black autumn berries and glorious foliage, handsome native; light not dense shade.	Clings to a trellis with own tendrils but requires a hefty one, drapes gracefully over stone walls; also good groundcover for slopes, as here.
tricuspidata Boston-ivy	50	D	Rampant, for light not dense shade; 3-lobed leaves (same as poison-ivy); good city vine; fine fall color.	Two miniature less-rampant growers are 'Lowii' and 'Beverly Brooks'. Clings naturally to stonework or to trees. Better not to plant next wood.

Polygonum aubertii Silverlace-vine	20–30	D	Fast-growing to 25 feet in one summer; strong woody vine that twines and clambers in semishade. Fragrant white panicles Aug.–Sept.	Almost took over this house even in western shade. Good for chain-link or other fence not against house; excellent to "roof" a heavy arbor.
Porcelain-vine, see *Ampelopsis*				
Silverlace-vine, see *Polygonum*				
Virginia-creeper, see *Parthenocissus*				
Wintercreeper, see *Euonymus*				
Woodbine, see *Parthenocissus*				

This shaded city garden designed in the Japanese manner features sections of brick paving set in white pebbles as a groundcover. English ivy on the wall, evergreen euonymus over the gate, Boston-ivy beyond it, ferns in the beds with Japanese pieris, and two pots of fiddle-leaf rubber plants (from indoors) at the entrance give this garden a unique charm. GEORGE TALOUMIS PHOTO

12

SHADE IN THE CITY

How to Cope and Be Glad

Shade in the country and shade in the city are similar but certainly not the same. Too often the city garden, surrounded by tall buildings or encompassed by a board fence, suffers two ills—poor air circulation and pollution. This doesn't mean that living in a shaded city location you can't have a garden; it does mean, if you are smart, that you will be aware of limitations, evaluate what you have, then design and plant accordingly.

What Tree?

Perhaps an ailanthus tree hovers above you. Respect it; it may be called a weed tree, but nicely pruned it gives you shifting light and a green canopy under which so much pleasant living is possible. Of course, if it is a male tree, those yellow June flowers will hardly suggest a perfume factory and you will have to cope as best you can, perhaps cutting off most of them with an extension pruner. But you may be lucky, as I have been here where the ailanthus tree is a well-behaved female. Or the weed tree in your city yard may be a box-elder, mulberry, silver maple, or white poplar. I found most of these in the wild at my own place in the country, also sassafras. With proper pruning, all became respectable ornamentals, though not in the lawn area. Whatever tree comes with your city place, I feel sure it can be an asset if you care to make it so with severe pruning at the start.

Design

In the city garden of limited area, good design is essential. On the wise use of space depend both good looks and comfort. If you expect to stay where you are for a couple of years or longer, it might be practical for you to have a landscape architect or designer draw up a plan for your guidance. In some cities there are firms that are more than simply florists who, in addition to plants, offer the kind of service you need.

If you are going to do the designing yourself, I suggest a path leading from a main door to the end of the area where the eye will be drawn to some feature, perhaps a handsome piece of stone, a statue, maybe a simple birdbath or sundial, if there is a little sun. Such an arrangement gives a pleasing sense of distance. The path could be of crushed stone, white quartz perhaps if it is to be important, flagstone laid in wood chips, or even concrete rounds. To decide on the best placement for your path, study your garden from a doorway or house window that looks out upon it. Then lay hose lengths for a trial run; this will help you check the placement.

Beds or Containers

On each side plan your flower beds, preferably raised ones, 18 to 24 inches deep, and retained by redwood sections or the more ele-

A great maple tree shades this paved and fenced city garden that adjoins the living room to make a delightful indoor-outdoor unit when glass doors are open in summer. At right, under the dogwood (growing over from the neighbor's garden) a dwarf Alberta spruce flourishes; a tall yew is espaliered against the wall; potted plants make nice accents. In spring tall white lily-flowered tulips bloom in the bed around the tree trunk, the bulbs discarded later. CHARLES MARDEN FITCH PHOTO

gant brick. Improve the soil with quantities of humus and top-dress the beds with fine peat moss. Trying to do anything with the existing soil is likely to be heartbreak. If you are both strong and optimistic, you can excavate 2 feet, remove the sick acid mess and replace it with good soil, but it's a lot easier to buy enough good soil for a raised bed. Here you can set out plants known to have city-endurance, as various ferns, hostas, daylilies, myrtle, ivies, and some bulbs, as scillas. For a grand effect, plant the lovely lily-flowered tulips, not for keeps but just for a handsome May effect. Lift and discard these bulbs, or give them away after they bloom. I know city gardeners who use white tulips most effectively in this expensive way. Annually purchased young plants of *Impatiens, Vinca rosea, Nicotiana, Coleus,* and *Caladium* will make a good display.

Raised beds of enriched soil mixed with humus are supported by flagstone sections. In the shade of neighboring trees, a big rhododendron flanked by dwarf spruces rises from a bed of green pachysandra and white flowering impatiens. CHARLES MARDEN FITCH PHOTO

Or you can give up the whole idea of much direct planting and put your all into container plants. Simply set these in pots or tubs (large enough not to freeze solid in winter) on top of the soil and spread a mulch around them for a neat effect. Two annuals that won't cost much even in quantity are impatiens and wax begonias, readily available in spring as well-started plants. Potted, they will bloom all summer and then make good window plants. In the fall some of your other outdoor plants can be brought indoors, depending on space and light there; evergreens outdoors in tubs defy the winter, and you will find even one red-berried yew or cotoneaster tipped with snow a very pleasing sight. Of course, some of your potted plants must simply go to plant heaven. In this matter of potted and boxed material, you will find excellent ideas and procedures in *Container Gardening Outdoors* by George Taloumis (Simon & Schuster, 1972).

Meanwhile have a look at these lists of trees, shrubs, groundcovers, vines, and perennials that have proved their vitality under city conditions of shade without sunshine. Planted in decent soil, either directly or in large containers, hose-sprayed daily or oftener (*be sure of a forceful stream*) during the growing season to wash off soot and discourage pests, and fertilized with soluble all-purpose plant food at almost every watering, all these plants should thrive and please you in your own shaded city garden.

But mine is a superficial treatment. Gardening in the city deserves a whole book, and I suggest for your further information Jack Kramer's *Your City Garden* (Charles Scribner's Sons, 1972) and *The City Gardener* by Philip Truex (Alfred A. Knopf, 1964).

PLANTS FOR CITY CONDITIONS

Small Trees

Amelanchier canadensis (Serviceberry)
Chionanthus virginicus (Fringetree)
Cornus mas (Cornelian-cherry)
Halesia carolina (Carolina Silverbell)
Pyrus calleryana 'Bradford' (Bradford Pear)

Evergreen Shrubs

Buxus microphylla japonica (Japanese or Littleleaf Boxwood)
Cotoneaster horizontalis (Rockspray Cotoneaster;
    semievergreen)
Euonymus fortunei (Wintercreeper)
Ilex crenata microphylla (Japanese Holly)
        glabra (Inkberry)
Leucothoe
Pieris floribunda (Mountain Andromeda)
        japonica (Japanese Andromeda)
Taxus cuspidata (Japanese Yew)

Deciduous Shrubs

Abelia grandiflora (Glossy Abelia)
Azalea vaseyi (Pinkshell Azalea)
Deutzia gracilis (Slender Deutzia)
Forsythia x *intermedia* (Forsythia)
Kerria japonica (Japanese Kerria)
Spiraea x *vanhouttei* (Vanhoutte Spirea)

Perennials and Bulbs

Crocus (Dutch Hybrids)
Dicentra eximia (Plumy Bleedingheart)
Hemerocallis (Daylily)

Hosta (Plaintain-lily)
Iris cristata (Crested Iris)
    verna (Spring Iris)
Scilla sibirica (Siberian squill)
    hispanica (Spanish Bluebell)
Tulipa (Tulips)
Viola (Violets)

Groundcovers

Ajuga reptans (Bugleweed)
Convallaria (Lily-of-the-Valley)
Epimedium (Barrenwort)
Hedera helix (English Ivy)
Pachysandra terminalis (Japanese Spurge)
Rosa wichuraiana (Memorial Rose)
Sedum acre (Goldmoss Stonecrop)
Vinca minor (Periwinkle)

Vines

Parthenocissus quinquefolia (Virginia Creeper)
    tricuspidata (Boston-ivy)
Polygonum aubertii (Silverlace-vine)
Wisteria floribunda (Japanese Wisteria;
  no bloom without sun)

Ferns

Osmunda cinnamomea (Cinnamon Fern)
    claytoniana (Interrupted Fern)
Polystichum acrostichoides (Christmas Fern)

The fast-growing honeylocust, *Gleditsia triacanthos,* is a choice shade tree, sifting the sunlight through its ferny leaves and thrusting roots deep enough for various evergreens and a lawn to thrive beneath it. In summer the shadow it casts is lovely to look upon.
GEORGE TALOUMIS PHOTO

13

IF YOU NEED SHADE

*Wonderful Chance
to Select the Best Trees*

What an opportunity you have to exactly suit yourself if you have bought a place with not a shade or flowering tree in sight. That's what I did and though I would have broiled the first summer without awnings, I had the chance you now have to select from the best possible big shade trees and the loveliest of the smaller flowering kinds. But don't set out just any tree because you are in such need. Trees are a permanent part of your place; the right trees will enhance it; the wrong ones detract and perhaps be a nuisance as well if they have habits of shredding or seeding.

What to Look For

Consider certain characteristics: size, rate of growth, shape, type of rooting (deep for a lawn tree), maybe pollution endurance, length of life (though I've always figured any tree will outlive me), and of course beauty of bloom, foliage, and autumn color. It's a good idea, too, to take thought as to neatness. Maybe littering is worth enduring in view of compensating values. I willingly tolerate a messy month after the fragrant fringetree blooms at the front door, and I'm not disturbed by the prickly sweetgum balls that must occasionally be raked up from the lawn, or the eternity of dried seedpods from the silverbell.

One thing none of us wants on the lawn is a shade tree with surface roots as those of Norway maple, beech, sycamore (buttonwood), poplar, and that horror of plumbers, the weeping willow. With the deep-rooters like the ash, honeylocust, red oak, white oak, sugar maple, sweetgum, tulip-tree, and yellow-wood, you can quite easily have shade and a flower garden too. Of course, you can achieve flowers even under a Norway maple but it's uphill work and there's no use inviting trouble by selecting it. If it comes along with your property, that's something else again.

As you walk the nursery rows—which is the only way to select anything as important and permanent as a tree—keep in mind that the small specimens you see may have mighty genes and are unlikely to have the same shape in maturity as they do now in youth. Try to see mature specimens of the ones that appeal most and grow well in properties like yours. If yours is a fairly small back yard, maybe 50 to 60 feet, you absolutely can't have a sugar maple, a white oak, an ash, and a tulip-tree, even if you have loved them all since childhood; each one of these needs at least a 40-foot spread, and space for the sun to reach beyond them for your flowers. You also can't have a couple of dogwoods, a crab apple, a magnolia, and a mountain-ash, even if you've admired them for years and have looked forward to the day when you'd have a place of your own where you could enjoy them all.

How Many for Your Place?

What you can have, artistically and comfortably, is one handsome shade tree and two, maybe three, small flowering trees, depending on what else your yard must provide, like a play space for children or a rather large area for parking. If yours is a bigger lot, say 100 to 150 feet, there you can have two fine shade trees and maybe five smaller flowering trees, and so on, more or less arithmetically. In any case, you want to shade your house not shroud it, and you probably want open space in the sun for flowers.

To help you in your maybe bitter choice, I have prepared these limited charts, practically with prayer and fasting, for the more trees I know, the more trees I love, and perhaps you are the same way. It may help to study the chart of big trees at the end of this chapter and of smaller flowering trees at the end of Chapter 10. (True, the smaller trees are recommended for shaded situations, but almost all enjoy the sun as well.) Study a couple of well-illustrated catalogues to help you prepare a limited list before you fare forth on your nursery safari.

If I were limited to one shade tree, I think it would be a thornless locust or a zelkova, both casting lacy shade and cool shadows. The sweetgum and tulip-tree would come next. Among the smaller shade trees, I'd favor the Japanese maple, Christmas-berry, and the English May-tree. For flowers, I'd have to have the fringetree, silverbell, and one of the smaller crab apples. Then where would I put a dogwood?

Having beaten down your enthusiasms, consider next *where* your trees should go. Usually it is essential to mitigate the glare at the southeast corner of your house, but the sun at the west can also be pretty hot so perhaps that's where you need shade most. It depends, of course, on how your house stands on your property, also where you live most in it. If you have a terrace where you like to sit in the afternoon, you must have shade there and preferably a tree that does not litter it with dead blossoms or big seedpods.

Well, anyway, it's fun to go tree shopping, and the more you know about trees beforehand, the better selections you will make. And you won't hurry for you *are* picking out something pretty permanent that you will look upon day-in, day-out, and, if you are wise now, always with pleasure in the future.

TALL DECIDUOUS TREES FOR SHADE AND BEAUTY

Beech, Norway and some other maples, poplars, and willows are not suggested here for lawn trees because they are shallow-rooted; neither lawns nor flower beds are likely to thrive under them.

Name	Height in Feet	Growth	Shape	Remarks
Acer saccharum Sugar Maple	90–100	Allow 50–60-foot space; slow to moderate, won't endure pollution.	Oval to round top; fairly deep-rooted; broad-leaved shrubs and myrtle thrive under mine; native, eastern North America.	Yellow, orange, scarlet fall coloring is the glory of New England. Remove branches to 12–15 feet above ground. (Avoid Norway, silver, box-elder, maples on lawns.)
Ash, see *Fraxinus*				
Betula papyrifera Canoe Birch	50–80	Grows fast, whitest bark of all the birches.	Narrow, rounded at top, native.	Most popular birch because not so susceptible to borers, but I like the pendulous European birch better and spray accordingly.

pendula European Birch	45	Grows fairly fast, fine white, black-barred trunk, smaller leaves than canoe birch, same golden autumn color.	Oval form, deep-rooted, with graceful drooping lateral branches, choice lawn tree here; allow 25-foot spread.	Here this is pruned open enough for me to look through to paths and plantings beyond.
Birch, sees *Betula*				
Cercidiphyllum japonicum Katsura-tree	40–60	Fast, good for tall screening at edge of property instead of Lombardy poplar; shallow-rooted, not for main lawn area.	Several trunks or pruned to one; needs rich moist soil.	Fine-textured foliage, pink tint to unfolding leaves, scarlet and gold in autumn.
Chinese Scholar-tree, see *Sophora japonica*				
Cladrastis lutea Yellow-wood	50–60	Allow 30–40-foot space. Medium fast, round-topped and spreading, move carefully in spring with root ball.	Deep-rooted, tolerant of poor soil; a choice tree; prune midsummer to fall, not spring; a bleeder.	Lovely native with white fragrant flowers like wisteria in spring; orange-yellow autumn foliage, gray bark.

Name	Height in Feet	Growth	Shape	Remarks
Dawn-redwood, see *Metasequoia*				
Fraxinus pennsylvanica lanceolata Green Ash	60	Fast-growing, leafs out late and leaves fall late.	Irregularly oval, grass grows well beneath it; good yellow autumn color; native, lovely on my lawn.	Plant pyramidal 'Marshall Seedless' to avoid seed nuisance. Here this is planted only 15 feet from sweetgum, the two mingling to give necessary shade from southern sun.
Ginkgo biloba Maidenhair-tree	60	Slow-growing.	Open, wide-spreading; fan-shaped leaves, gives lacy effect.	Makes a beautiful specimen; be sure of a male tree, very smelly fruits on females; brilliant yellow in fall.
Gleditsia triacanthos Honeylocust	125	Fast, among the very best.	High and open, gives light ferny shade; flowers and grass thrive beneath it; no autumn color; native.	Good for almost immediate effect. Select the thornless 'Inermis', 'Moraine', or 'Sunburst', with golden young leaves as if in bloom; casts beautiful shadows.

Honeylocust,
see *Gleditsia*

Katsura-tree,
see *Cercidiphyllum*

Larch, see *Larix*

Larix decidua European Larch	100	Fast, for well-drained soils.	Pyramidal in youth, spreading in age as branches droop.	Choice deciduous cone-bearer, a golden flame of needles in autumn before they drop; I prize this but larches are for edge of lawn not center.
laricina American Larch or Tamarack	60	Fast, for moist to wet soils.	Pyramidal and pendulous, native.	Notable hardiness even across northern Canada; common in New England marshy places; not so handsome as European.

Linden, see *Tilia*

Name	Height in Feet	Growth	Shape	Remarks
Liquidambar styraciflua Sweetgum	80	Moderate.	Broadly pyramidal, grass grows under mine; Eastern native.	Star-shaped leaves, glorious crimson autumn color; globular spiny fruits for Christmas decorations.
Liriodendron tulipifera Tulip-tree	70–100	Fast, long-lived, rich moist soil, prune in early summer.	Cylindrical; pale green-and-yellow tulip-shaped flowers, mid-June, native.	Deep-rooted; transplant with earth ball while small; handsome square dark leaves yellow fall color; thrives beside my brook, very beautiful.
Maple, see *Acer*				
Metasequoia glyptostroboides Dawn-redwood	50–60	Fast, prune away side branches to 8-9 feet, allow 30-foot spread.	Pyramidal, needs big planting hole; can be transplanted bare root.	Deep-rooted with amber autumn color; a rare deciduous cone-bearer but easy to grow.
Oak, see *Quercus*				
Pagoda-tree, see *Sophora*				

Quercus alba White Oak	100	Slow, dense foliage; allow 60–70 feet space.	Rounded, spreading, a noble tree, native.	Deep-rooted, volunteered here on top of cliff when an acorn probably dropped into a soil-filled crack; dark purplish red in fall.
palustris Pin Oak	80	Moderate, can spread to 35 feet.	Pyramidal, low branches drooping to ground; fine specimen native.	Fairly deep-rooted; brilliant red in fall, must be pruned high for a lawn tree.
rubra Red Oak	75	Fast and spreading; allow 50 feet.	Rounded, deep-rooted, native.	Dark-red fall foliage, not for small area.
Sassafras albidum Sassafras	60	Fast, deep root system, can be pruned to a fine specimen; mitten-shaped leaves.	Rounded, thrives in poor soil, weed tree here, suckers are easily transplanted, native. I like it.	Good for quick shade; yellow spring flowers, scarlet fall foliage; a second choice, I'd say.

Name	Height in Feet	Growth	Shape	Remarks
Sophora japonica Pagoda-tree, Scholar-tree	50–60	Needs 40-feet spread; slow to medium; won't tolerate wet sour soil.	Round-topped, deep-rooted; plant away from terrace or steps because of flower and fruit litter.	Creamy pealike flower cluster in August; evergreen effect in winter due to green bark and twig color; stands pollution; grass will grow under it.
Sweetgum, see *Liquidambar*				
Tamarack, see *Larix*				
Tilia cordata Littleleaf Linden or Lime	50–60	Slow, casts deep shade.	Symmetrical; pale yellow blooms June–July, scented particularly in early evening.	Small, heart-shaped leaves give nice texture effect to this European tree; endures pollution; favorite of aphids so don't plant next terrace.
Tulip-tree, see *Liriodendron*				
Yellow-wood, see *Cladrastis*				

Zelkova serrata Japanese Zelkova	50	Fast, many slender ascending branches.	Rounded top, short trunk; prune to avoid too thick growth.	This elm relative with lacy foliage planted here beside the brook to replace an elm casualty; lovely fall coloring yellow to bronze; a charming tree.

Suspended from a low branch of a fringetree at the front door and opposite the guest-room window, a hanging basket of fuchsias is a pretty sight for those who come in and those who stay. GEORGE TALOUMIS PHOTO

MISCELLANY

HANGING BASKETS AND
WINDOW BOXES IN SHADE

Among the most decorative additions to the summer garden are the graceful basket plants suspended from pergola or arbor beams or from a stout outreaching branch of a tree. As for window boxes filled with shade-preference flowering annuals, foliage plants, and vines, they can make a garden even at a north window if there is good light there.

I take special pleasure in trailing plants both indoors and out and so have a number of ferns—asparagus, rabbits-foot, and sprawling Bostons—and various tender trailers I like to see suspended from the arbor along the east side of the house. Only a little sunlight reaches them there due to the heavy wisteria foliage overhead, but it is enough and they are protected from wind there which is so essential for hanging plants outdoors. Then a strong propitious branch of the fringetree at the front door makes an ideal support for a fuchsia one year, an Italian bellflower (*Campanula isophylla*) another, or one of my gesneriads—achimenes, columnea, or episcia. My big green-and-white spider plant (*Chlorophytum*) was born to be a basket plant with its 3-foot leaf extension ending in new little clustered plants. A white wax begonia, overflowing a pot set on a pedestal indoors, makes a charming complement for a green door outside, the pot securely ensconced in a plastic basket (hidden by the plant) and suspended from a birdcage hanger.

I do not transfer my valuable house plants to wire baskets but rather set the pots in redwood or other hanging containers with a packing of peat moss to retard drying out.

Various flowering annuals that like half-and-half shade make delightful, even dramatic, plants for hanging containers. I think of impatiens cultivars—pink, red, orange, or white—preferably the 6- to 12-inch growers that will soon sprawl over the edge of a basket. I like the annual periwinkle, *Vinca rosea,* white or rose; the trailing yellow-to-orange black-eyed Susan-vine; blue and white browallias (see Color Section); white-throated cardinal-climber; and the white or rose cypress-vine. Sow seeds of these indoors late in February to have blooming plants for your baskets in May; most of them are not available as started plants, except impatiens and perhaps browallia. Of course, none of these is for more than half-shade; in deeper shade you will get hardly any bloom.

A vine is usually essential to fill out a basket planting with an upright plant in the center, as a light-blue browallia. A small-leaved English ivy will look nice around this or one of the so-called ivies, as the German (*Senecio*) or Swedish (*Plectranthus*), and you may have all of these in your window garden for this pleasing outdoor use.

Then there are the trailing tuberous begonias. Perhaps these are the handsomest of all basket plants and worthy of prominent display, and alone, but definitely not in deep shade and with reliable wind protection.

Outdoors hanging plants need an unconscionable amount of water I find even when peat moss is mulched around the pots or used liberally in the potting medium. Keep this in mind as you hang them, particularly if you are of low stature like me. I keep a stepstool near the kitchen door and there are days when I have to climb it more than once.

If you plant your baskets yourself (and I may say I prefer to let the florist or grower do this while I stand idly by full of advice), you will need well-moistened sphagnum moss or a sheet of green woods moss for a liner. For soil the balanced house plant Equal Thirds medium will be fine—garden loam, compost (brown peat is fine), and coarse sand. I water my basket plants just as I do my house plants adding a *little* soluble fertilizer each time, preferably a kind low in nitrogen, high in phosphorus, as one of the Peters brands or Hyponex, with Miracid for the ferns.

Window Boxes

The kind of plants you select for window boxes in light shade or full light will be about the same as for baskets. Some years I have filled a window box with house plants. These are not planted directly, of course; instead, pots are retained and packed in peat moss to prevent swift drying out.

In window boxes you will want trailing plants only for the edgings, upright growers for the main effect. Tuberous begonias alone of one color or in combination are beautiful, and green-and-white caladiums with variegated ivy or a white-striped inch-plant (*Tradescantia albiflora*) are an effective combination.

For the upright growers select medium-tall impatiens, semper-florens begonias, or other plants that attract you at a roadside market or garden center. Only, remember, don't fall for the sun-lovers like geraniums; they *must* have sun and will be a real fizzle at your sunless north window, and petunias also need some sun. In a half-and-half location you will probably get fair bloom from the smaller varieties.

HERBS IN SHADE

Perhaps growing herbs except in dry, sunny places is a contradiction in your mind. You think of herbs not only as sun-lovers but also sun-demanding. Yet a number of them have proved they will do well in half-and-half shade, that is, with morning or afternoon sun, or under trees like the honeylocust where the sunlight is filtered.

The mints, of course, are not in the least particular. In a quite deep shady corner, I thought to raise a patch of mint to cut for summer drinks; what I got was not a patch but a takeover. Sweet woodruff, one of my favorite groundcovers, requires both shade and moisture, as do most of the plants listed below, and for May wine the leaves of sweet woodruff are essential. If you like to make unusual confections, you can crystalize the stems of angelica and the rootstalks of wild ginger, for you can grow both plants in the shade.

Here are some herbs for a shady area where the soil is pleasingly moist and fertility is assured.

Bay leaf	Lovage
Burnet	Marjoram
Chervil	Mints
Costmary	Oregano
Curly Parsley	Sweet Cicely
English Pennyroyal	Tarragon
Lemon Balm	Winter Savory

FOR THE BIRDS—BERRIES, A GARDEN ASSET

If you are interested in birds and want to make your place attractive to them without the great do of a sanctuary planting, select some of the trees and shrubs that offer vivid summer-to-winter crops of berries and also flourish in light shade. In the fruiting stage, many plants are as colorful as when they are in bloom, so by growing these you please not only many birds but also yourself.

It is amusing to see how fast the soft juicy berries are stripped from trees and shrubs; in fact, you scarcely see the crop before it is gone on the Cornelian-cherry, barberry, fruiting yews at your doorway, cotoneaster, shadbush, and the early-fruiting viburnums, as the European cranberry-bush (*V. opulus*) and the doublefile (*V. plicatum tomentosum*). The fruits that linger, drier kinds I suppose, are left until hunger is greater, taste less fastidious. From late fall into winter, you may still see colorful fruits on your hawthorn, privet, hollies, dogwoods, bayberry, snowberry, red chokeberry, winterberry, mountain-ash, American cranberry-bush, and on vines like Boston-ivy and Virginia-creeper.

Of course, a mulberry tree will attract even more than cherries, and my mulberry is pretty much shaded by a maple, but I haven't included this wild tree in my recommendations because the fruit is on the messy side falling on a driveway and on the roofs of cars. Planted where it isn't a nuisance, the mulberry offers an early summer treat to many birds, as orioles and thrushes, not just the robins and bluejays, which are far from particular.

TREES AND SHRUBS WITH BERRIES

Amelanchier canadensis	Shadbush
Aronia arbutifolia	Red Chokeberry
Berberis sp.	Barberry
Cornus sp.	Dogwood
Cotoneaster sp.	
Crataegus sp.	Hawthorn
Ilex sp.	Holly
Lindera benzoin	Spicebush
Malus sp. and var.	Crab Apple

Mitchella repens	Partridge-berry
Parthenocissus quinquefolia	Virginia-creeper
tricuspidata	Boston-ivy
Sambucus sp.	Elder
Skimmia	
Sorbus sp.	Mountain-ash
Symphoricarpus sp.	Snowberry
Taxus sp.	Yew
Viburnum sp.	

SHADE-INTO-SUN SITUATIONS

When a flower border stretches from a shaded area, perhaps under trees, to a sunny open area beyond, you have to take thought as to what will prosper under both conditions if you are to have a pleasing continuity. Right off, an uninterruped edging plant is important. Performing well under both conditions, it will give unity. Even if there are quite different plants behind it—though there needn't be—a well-chosen edging plant saves the day.

The three I have used for this purpose are the hardy evergreen candytuft, *Iberis sempervirens,* the wide species, though the smaller cultivars like 'Purity' and 'Autumn Snow' will do as well; rosy coral-bells, *Heuchera sanguinea,* or a chartreuse, red, or white cultivar, the colorful mats of foliage in evidence except in the dead of winter; and the evergreen myrtle, *Vinca minor,* not vining but clipped to make a little hedge. I might suggest a pretty fourth, the ferny lavender Jacobs-ladder, *Polemonium reptans,* and I have used it often, only it takes an early summer vacation after the long spring bloom and the plants almost disappear.

Behind the continuous shade-to-sun edging, the early spring bulbs, right up to the May tulips, will bloom well throughout the border. You can then conceal their departure with plants of the new F-1 hybrid fibrous begonias, strains of *B. semperflorens,* pale and deep pink or white, that are available from Wayside Gardens and bloom in *full sun* as well as shade.

If your shaded section is under a tree, you might make a mass planting there of ferns brightened with bulbs and a colorful edging. If considerable light comes through, a number of perennials will bloom there as well as beyond in the sun, though not so heavily. You will be bound to get excellent progression if you select some astilbes, balloon-flowers, daylilies, globeflowers, meadowrue (*Thalictrum glaucum*), physostegia, the new tradescantias, or windflowers throughout. Then if you wish, you could have some variation—bleedinghearts and hostas only in the shaded area, chrysanthemums and phlox only in the sun. And what a handsome spring-to-fall border you will have with no severe break from shade to sun.

SHADE WITH POOR DRAINAGE

If you have poor drainage along with shade, you have a pretty limited situation. You can take one of two courses: Accept the dampness and select plants that naturally endure this, or correct the drainage. On a fair-sized property where only a small area stays wet, you can have fun with a little bog planting like mine across the brook where the marsh-marigolds are such bright harbingers of spring and certain ferns thrive with wet feet.

In a *somewhat* damp location, a considerable number of trees, shrubs, and perennials will do well, and I have listed some of these below. However, most plants need a certain amount of air around the roots and will die if the standing water *never* drains off.

If your whole place is poorly drained, I think you really have no choice but to install, or have installed by an *experienced* contractor, drainage tiles and pipes to carry off excess water and so leave you a healthy place with conditions that promote good gardening. This drainage improvement is not an inexpensive procedure but so basic you have to consider it.

PLANTS FOR RATHER WET PLACES

Trees

Acer rubrum	Swamp Maple
Alnus	Alder
Ilex sp.	Hollies
Larix laricina	Eastern Larch
Liquidambar styraciflua	Sweetgum
Magnolia virginiana	Sweetbay Magnolia
Salix sp.	Willows
Thuja occidentalis	American Arborvitae

Shrubs

Amelanchier	Shadblow
Andromeda	
Aronia	Red Chokeberry
Calluna vulgaris	Heather
Calycanthus floridus	Strawberry-shrub
Clethra alnifolia	Summersweet
Gaylussacia brachycera	Box-huckleberry
Ilex glabra	Inkberry
verticillata	Winterberry
Kalmia latifolia	Mountain-laurel
Leucothoe fontanesiana (*catesbaei*)	Drooping Leucothoe
Lindera benzoin	Spicebush
Myrica pensylvanica	Bayberry
Rhododendron (including Azalea)	
arborescens	Sweet Azalea
canadense	Rhodora
nudiflorum	Pinxterbloom
maximum	Rosebay
vaseyi	Pinkshell Azalea
viscosum	Swamp Azalea

Rosa palustris	Swamp Rose
Salix descolor	Pussy Willow
Sambucus canadensis	American Elder
Vaccinium corymbosum	Highbush Blueberry
Viburnum carlcephalum	Fragrant Snowball
cassinoides	Witherod
trilobum .	American Cranberry-bush

Perennials

Acorus calamus	Sweet Flag
Althaea officinalis	Marshmallow
Asarum europaeum	Wild Ginger
Asclepias incarnata	Swamp Milkweed
Asperula odorata	Sweet Woodruff
Aster novae-angliae	New England Aster
Astilbe sp.	Astilbe
Bergenia cordifolia	Heartleaf Bergenia
Caltha palustris	Marsh-marigold
Cimicifuga racemosa	Snakeroot
Erica carnea	Spring Heather
Eupatorium maculatum	Joe-Pye-weed
Ferns, for bogs	
Athyrium filix-femina	Lady Fern
Dryopteris spinulosa	Toothed Wood Fern
Onoclea sensibilis	Sensitive Fern
Osmunda cinnamomea	Cinnamon Fern
claytonia	Interrupted Fern
regalis	Royal Fern
Helenium autumnale	Common Sneezeweed
Iris pseudacorus	Iris, Yellow Flag
versicolor	Blue Flag
Lathyrus palustris	Marsh Pea
Lilium canadense	Canada Lily
superbum	Turkscap Lily
Lobelia cardinalis	Cardinal-flower

Lysimachia clethroides	Japanese Loosestrife
Monarda didyma	Beebalm
Myosotis palustris	True Forget-Me-Not
Primula japonica	Japanese Primrose
Ranunculus	Buttercup
Trollius sp.	Globeflower
Valeriana officinalis	Garden-heliotrope
Viola blanda	Sweet White Violet
cucullata	Common Blue Violet

SOURCES OF PLANTS, SEEDS,
AND SUPPLIES

This could be an endless list for we are blessed in this country with many fine nurseries and mail-order houses. Here are just a few of which I have special knowledge; all publish catalogues (price indicated where a charge). For good service, get your orders in early.

Mail Order

Blackthorne Gardens, 48 Quincy Street, Holbrook, Massachusetts 02343 . . . lilies (will store bulb orders till spring).

W. Atlee Burpee Co., Philadelphia, Pennsylvania 19132 . . . general, flower seeds, grass seed for shade, some nursery stock.

P. deJager & Sons, South Hamilton, Massachusetts 01982 . . . bulbs.

Girard Nurseries, Geneva, Ohio 44041 . . . trees and shrubs; azaleas and rhododendrons.

Lamb Nurseries, E. 101 Sharp Avenue, Spokane, Washington 99202 . . . ferns and wildflowers; shrubs, vines, groundcovers, herbs.

Leslie's Wild Flower Nursery, 30 Summer Street, Methuen, Massachusetts 01844 . . . ferns and wildflowers; plants and seed; 25¢.

Charles H. Mueller, River Road, New Hope, Pennsylvania 18938 . . . bulbs.

Geo. W. Park Seed Co., Greenwood, South Carolina 29646 . . . flower seeds, grass seed for shade, some rarities; summer bulbs, ornamental grasses.

Putney Nursery, Inc., Putney, Vermont 05346 . . . wildflowers and ferns; herbs, some general nursery stock; 25¢.

Louis Smirnow, 85 Linden Lane, Glen Head P.O., Brookville, Long Island, New York 11545 . . . tree peonies. Catalogue in color.

The Tingle Nursery Co., Pittsville, Maryland 21850 . . . trees and shrubs, large selection, azaleas, hollies.

Vick's Wildgardens, Inc., Box 115, Gladwyne, Pennsylvania 19035 . . . ferns and wildflowers.

Wayside Gardens, Mentor, Ohio 44060 . . . general; handsomest of catalogues; wide selection of fine varieties, good shade section. Catalogue in color, $2, refundable with orders.

White Flower Farm, Litchfield, Connecticut 06759 . . . general; excellent *Garden Book* with good cultural advice; many rarities. Spring and Fall editions of *The Garden Book,* plus three issues of *Notes,* are sold annually by subscription for $3. Orders of $15.00 or more, no charge for publications.

To Visit

Martin Viette Nurseries, Northern Boulevard (25A), East Norwich, Long Island, New York, 11732 . . . Excellent *Perennial & Shrub Handbook-Catalogue,* cultural guide for shade plantings, notes on individual plants, 50¢.

Oliver Nurseries, 1159 Bronson Road, Fairfield, Connecticut 06430 . . . Rhododendrons, azaleas, pines, rock garden evergreens.

INDEX

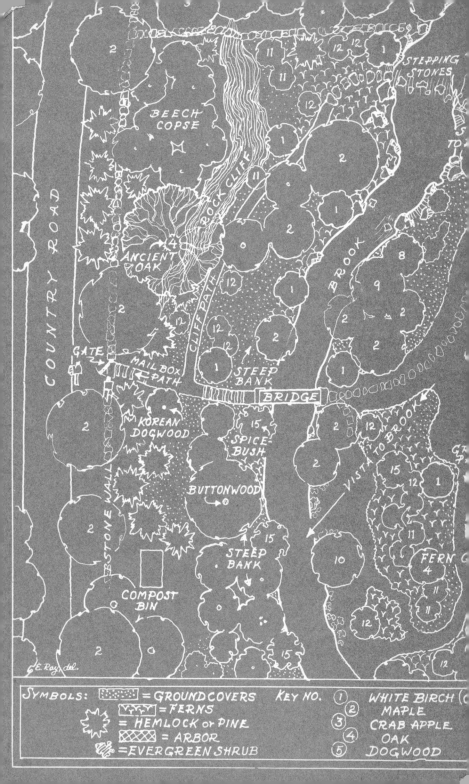

SYMBOLS: ▒▒▒▒ = GROUND COVERS   KEY NO.   ① WHITE BIRCH
🌿 ᵛᵛᵛ = FERNS   ② MAPLE
= HEMLOCK or PINE   ③ CRAB APPLE
⨯⨯⨯ = ARBOR   ④ OAK
= EVERGREEN SHRUB   ⑤ DOGWOOD